Soul Mates: Path to a Praying Partnership is a book about the power of prayer within a marriage. It is also about two people who discovered how loving Jesus first and best empowers them to love one another more fully and follow Christ more intentionally. Nick and Mary Portzen write with humility, wonder, and frankness about how praying together helps them repent of sins and be more grateful for their blessings. Bible reading and biblical thinking saturates every page of this book, from the verses that begin and end each chapter to the questions and exercises for couples to ponder and complete. *Soul Mates* is for every couple, from newlyweds to those married for decades, who want to use prayer to put Christ at the center of their lives and their relationship.

—**Jolene Philo**, national speaker and coauthor of *Sharing Love Abundantly in Special Needs Families: The 5 Love Languages® for Parents Raising Children with Disabilities*

With transparency and wisdom gained through their experiences, the Portzens write about the results of welcoming God into their relationship. Sharing from their own perspectives, they offer helpful insights and show how praying together in a genuine, conversational way as a couple united them spiritually, brought intimacy to their marriage, and strengthened their bond with God. Not only do Mary and Nick include questions for discussion at the end of each easy-to-read chapter, but they also weave in writing prompts and ideas for prayer. Their book is an excellent resource for couples who want to transform their marriages and individual lives.

—**Twila Belk**, author, speaker, conference presenter (www.gottatellsomebody.com)

My husband and I have been married for more than twenty-five years, and we have loved Jesus the whole time. But it's only been in the past few years, after being hit with multiple life-altering circumstances, not the least of which was my second breast cancer battle, that we decided to get on our knees together instead of separately. And goodness has it been a blessing. I'm convinced that *Soul Mates: Path to a Praying Partnership* will give other couples a starting point for this valuable step toward more intimacy with both spouse and Savior.

—**Kim Harms**, author of *Life Reconstructed: Navigating the World of Mastectomies and Breast Reconstruction* (2021) and *Carried Through Cancer: 70 Days of Spiritual Strength from Cancer Fighters, Survivors and Caregivers* (Lifeway 2025)

"We hope something in this book has convinced you to give prayer a chance to do incredible things for your marriage, whether you've been married fifty years or five months," Mary Portzen said in this book. And these words are exactly what I thought while reading *Soul Mates: Path to a Praying Partnership.* Every couple can learn amazing truths when they commit to praying. This book is a gem of multiple opportunities to explore while on the path of prayer in marriage. Be open. Be brave. Be willing to listen. Like the quote from this book states, give prayer a chance. Incredible things will happen if you do.

—**Mary Jedlicka Humston**, writer, poet, and coauthor of *Mary & Me: A Lasting Link Through Ink*

SOUL MATES

SOUL MATES

Path to a *Praying* Partnership

NICK & MARY
PORTZEN

WOODNEST
PUBLISHING

Soul Mates: Path to a Praying Partnership

Published by Woodnest Publishing
ISBN: 9798218531690

Editing, cover, and book design by Michelle Rayburn

Cover art and back cover photo by Emily Miles © Emily Rose Artistry

Contents

Introduction

"Don't you think praying together is one of the most intimate experiences a couple can experience?" The question was rhetorical, as the person who said it had no real intention of praying with their spouse.

Why not?

Nick and I have a theory. Praying together requires vulnerability, and we humans aren't very good at being vulnerable. Additionally, too few of us have observed the example of a couple holding hands and talking to God together.

Yet, what if we told you that with one simple step you can up the level of your marriage from ordinary to *extraordinary*? In this book, Nick and I maintain that praying together is that one thing.

Are you willing to try it? It's free. And easy—once you get past the initial awkwardness. And dare we say it? We guarantee the practice will improve your marriage.

Men, maybe you were dragged, kicking and screaming, to this book by your wife. For that reason, my manly man husband has opened his heart to speak his mind and include the male perspective on each of the topics to speak directly to you.

For clarification, when Nick and I use the term "Christian," we aren't talking about a particular religion. Instead, we mean someone who not only believes in God but is a follower of

Jesus Christ. If you don't know the difference, we trust that you will by the end of this book.

Jesus is the one true way to heaven. You can follow Him with or without your spouse. From our own personal experience, we maintain that growing in faith together is an incredible experience. The cover of this book features a painting created by my daughter, Emily Rose Miles, of Emily Rose Artistry, depicting what we imagine as our shared journey on the path to heaven.

As for the term "soul mate" in our title, we aren't using the world's definition of soul mate but a biblical one that denotes a spiritual union, one that includes husband, wife, and God. Our prayer for you is that as you read through this book, you discover that same deep intimacy in your marriage as we have in ours.

Mary Portzen

Chapter 1

In the Beginning

"For I know the plans I have for you," declares the Lord, "plans to prosper you and not to harm you, plans to give you hope and a future."

Jeremiah 29:11

Mary:

Where was I in my spiritual journey on a summer day in 2018 when I heard the prompting of the Holy Spirit? Widowed six years before, I'd learned to trust God's guidance, to hear His voice.

I was one month into my new job as a program coordinator at a spirituality center, having recently moved with my youngest daughter an hour away from the only support system I had: my seven adult children, my sisters, and a Bible study group that had gathered bi-weekly in my home for the previous three years.

I was alone in the car on the way to work when I heard the distinct directive. *Pray for him.* The message was clear—and urgent. I was to pray for someone immediately.

Pray for him. The words came more insistent. Who? Who was I supposed to be praying for?

Your future husband.

My heart skipped a beat, my breath catching in my throat. There was a husband in my future? I shrugged off the prompting, not quite daring to believe that possibility. I'd given up on ever finding love again, though there was no denying I desired it. I was incredibly lonely. How I yearned to have someone to hug, hold hands with, to love, and be loved by.

I'm ashamed to admit I didn't immediately obey the divine summons, wrestling with the urgent request until I couldn't ignore the prompt any longer. On the morning of July 25, 2018, I opened my journal and wrote out a prayer for my future husband. Knowing the man must be going through a tough time, I prayed that he had friends and family as a support system along with a faith to hang on to. I promptly covered the prayer with a piece of paper, embarrassed by my vulnerability.

Over the next three years, I'd often wonder about that prompting. Loneliness exacerbated by the isolation of a pandemic, there were many nights I lay in the darkness of my bedroom, clutching a wooden comfort cross in my palm, crying out to God.

Where is this husband you promised me? I'd pray, my heart aching, tears streaming down my cheeks. Had I imagined the whole thing? By June 2021, I was at a low point when a good friend called me to ask how a recent date with a Christian man had gone.

"What is wrong with me?" I asked her. "Why couldn't I feel something more than warmth toward him? He's a good man. But as soon as we hugged, I just knew, without a doubt. He wasn't the one for me."

I explained how I'd asked God to protect my heart after my spouse's death, and He'd done so in obvious ways. It seemed God had answered my prayer for protection by shutting off a switch that had yet to be flipped back on.

"There's nothing wrong with you. You just haven't found the right one yet," my friend assured me. As a former minister, her advice was to pray specifically. "Make a list. Tell God exactly what you desire in a man."

I filled another page in my journal, listing the qualities I wanted in a husband. The ideal man would be seeking a deeper relationship with God. He'd make me laugh, and I'd be able to tell him anything. He would pray with me. He'd love my children. My list got very specific. He'd have kind eyes, broad shoulders, and a neatly trimmed goatee.

A few days later, I began corresponding online with a widower. When his first few messages revealed his desire to grow in faith, I agreed to meet with him. As Nick climbed the stairs to my doorstep, I noted his kind eyes, broad shoulders, and the neatly trimmed hair on his chin. We fell easily into conversation, talking as though we'd known each other forever, even sharing things we'd never shared with anyone before. It was as if our souls recognized each other.

It wasn't just a soul connection. As we hugged goodbye, I immediately recognized something different in my body's reaction to this man. As he turned to leave, I touched his arm, and he spun around to hug me again. We hugged once more at the door. Three hugs, and I knew, without a doubt, the switch God had turned off some nine years before had been flipped back on.

I soon learned I wasn't the only one who couldn't sleep that night, tossing and turning. At the break of dawn, we texted each other, wondering at the intensity of our feelings after just one meeting. I knew we needed to invite God into the relationship. We had to begin our next date with prayer.

I was nervous about asking Nick to pray with me. I'd learned to pray with other people in the almost ten years I'd been widowed—friends, colleagues, and fellow speakers before important events. But this would be the first time I'd pray with a man I was romantically interested in. I knew if he rejected the idea, he was not the man God meant for me, so I was relieved his answer was "Absolutely!"

Nick and I held hands for the first time as I prayed out loud, welcoming God into our relationship. I'm not sure we let go of each other for the next nine hours as we talked and laughed. When Nick shared that his wife had died in 2018, I felt a distinct prickle at the back of my neck.

That evening, Nick texted me. "I'm not sure what is happening. I know it's too soon, and I don't want to scare you, but I think I'm falling in love with you."

God had promised me a husband. He'd brought a man into my life who was everything I'd hoped for and more than I could have imagined. A man who made me laugh, who I could talk to about anything, one who loved holding hands and whose hugs left me weak in the knees, a man who was offering me love. How could this be?

I called my mentor, Cecil Murphey. Nearly thirty years older and widely published in the Christian book industry, Cec was more than a writing mentor. I often turned to him for spiritual advice.

"Mary, why are you surprised?" was Cec's reply. "This is exactly how it happens when God is in it from the beginning. Trust your feelings."

I was scared to trust my own feelings, but I had learned to trust God. It was obvious; Nick was God's answer to my prayers lamenting my loneliness.

The next time we met, I pulled out my 2018 journal. I showed Nick the covered entry, explaining I hadn't looked at it since I wrote it.

"I want to look at it with you," I said. My hands shaking a little with emotion, I carefully peeled back the paper I'd taped over the page.

"I've wrestled with God for a couple days since He asked me to pray for my future husband, but He wouldn't leave me alone, so here goes," I read, not daring to look up to see Nick's reaction. "Dear future husband," I continued, reading the entire prayer before meeting Nick's eyes, which were wet with unshed tears.

"That was the summer after my wife died, the worst summer of my life. Do you think that man you prayed for was me?" his hoarse whisper belied his emotions.

"I wouldn't have read it to you if I didn't think so," I whispered back.

Having both loved and lost someone, once we were certain it was God who'd brought us together, we didn't want to waste even one precious minute without the other. On August 23, 2021, three years after God asked me to pray for the man He'd promised me, surrounded by our twelve children and grandchildren, I married him. As part of the marriage vows, I read a section from the journal:

> *I'm praying that God brings us together in a way we will see Him in it. I pray that you already have a relationship with Him, that you are surrounded by family and friends who love you. I pray that we will grow in faith before we meet, as we get to know each other, and after we make a commitment to each other and to God, growing stronger in Him together. Finally, I pray that we glorify God in everything we do.*

Nick says:

I remember coming home from my first date with Mary and telling my daughter that I'd met the woman I was going to marry. I just knew.

I always wondered what was going on in my life, outside of the normal grieving process, when Mary felt prompted to pray for her future husband. I figured we'd never know since I didn't keep a journal or write things down like she did. We were married for almost two years before Mary thought to look up the date in my VA medical records. She discovered I'd tripped and fallen at the golf course around that time. On the day she prayed for me, I'd ended up in the ER because the pain had gotten so bad. That meant I had physical pain on top of the emotional pain of grieving a spouse, a real low point in my life. I still have a hard time believing that God had cared enough about me that He would prompt a stranger to pray for me!

DISCUSSION

Trust in the Lord *with all your heart and lean not on your own understanding; in all your ways submit to him, and he will make your paths straight.*

Proverbs 3:5–6

1. Mary talks about feeling a “soul connection” with Nick. Have you ever felt an immediate connection with someone? If so, who was it with? What did that connection mean to you?

2. What qualities do you think constitute a “soul connection” vs. the everyday encounters?

3. What about your relationship as a couple? Have you invited God into your marriage? If not, it is never too late. Following is a prayer to read aloud together to get the two of you started on this shared prayer journey.

Pray together:

Dear Lord, thank you for my spouse. We know that You have a perfect design for marriage, and we want our union to represent that. Please show us what You want for us as a couple and how to love each other in a way that honors You. Forgive us if we've lost sight of You or each other in the busyness of life. Please guide us to a new, improved relationship as we work our way through these chapters.

Chapter 2

What Is Prayer?

Whether you turn to the right or to the left, your ears will hear a voice behind you, saying, "This is the way; walk in it."

ISAIAH 30:21

Mary:

What is prayer exactly? If you'd asked either one of us that question before we experienced the death of a spouse, our answers likely would have been similar. Both raised in Catholic homes with the example of memorized, rote prayers like the Our Father and Hail Mary, we turned to the same format of prayer as adults while raising our respective families. Neither one of us recalls praying with our first spouse outside of prayer in church or perhaps a quick prayer under duress.

Between us, we had over seventy years of marriage under our belts when we met each other in 2021. One would assume we would know everything there was to know about commitment, communication, and the covenant of a marriage relationship. Yet in all those years with our first spouses, we'd never experienced the intimacy and power of praying together. We'd never held hands to pray out loud for our marriage or each other. We weren't even sure why or how to do that for ourselves until the darkness of our respective grief drove us down to our knees.

As for me, I believe my faith journey began with the legacy of faith my mother left behind when she died in 2010, on my fifty-first birthday. When my five-year-old grandson was diagnosed with cancer the following month, I grasped desperately on to the hope that my mother might be able to watch over him from heaven, a concept reinforced by Jacob himself when he'd say "Grandma" as he patted his right shoulder. I found myself looking heavenward during those turbulent times as Jacob underwent surgery, chemotherapy, and radiation. I believe now that God used that experience to prepare me to turn to Him when I lost my husband, David, a year and a half later.

After David's death, I was thrust into a state of stillness I'd never experienced before as a homeschooling mother of eight. I instinctively knew I needed God's Word along with the kind of praying I'd observed at a Christian writer's conference the summer before, where attendees talked about "hearing God" and "following Jesus." I hadn't understood their words at the time. What did they mean? God never talked to me. All I knew was they had something I desperately needed, a personal relationship with a God who guided them in their life.

The Bible tells us, "You will seek me and find me when you seek me with all your heart" (Jeremiah 29:13). I certainly did find God in those ensuing months, getting to know Him in the still, quiet moments of early morning as I prayed, journaled, and devoured devotionals and books penned by pastors and biblical scholars. Somehow, though I'd never read the Bible before, I intuitively knew the book held all the answers I needed. Yet, I wasn't sure how to find them.

When an editor asked if I would write ten devotions for a grief Bible, I readily agreed, even though I'd never written a devotion in my life. I knew the assignment would force me to delve into the Word of God. Once I started, I wanted more. The blind leading the blind, I formed a Bible study at my church. For the next five years, I studied the Bible with others who were hungry for God's direction. The more we read and studied, the closer we got to God. Not only did I learn how to pray in a genuine conversational way, but I also mastered the art of listening to the Holy Spirit, discerning a voice separate from my own.

"What does that mean, to hear God's voice?" others have asked. I explain it this way: You're in a grocery store and hear a distinctive peal of laughter an aisle or two away, immediately recognizing who it is because you know that laugh so well. Or you answer the phone and recognize the voice even before they identify themselves.

That's what happens when we get to know God through reading His Word. It isn't that we hear a booming voice from up above, but one inside our head, a thought we know didn't come from ourselves. We recognize it as God's because of our familiarity with Him. The voice *can* be loud, like a booming laugh two aisles over in the store. It was when I heard the urgent "Pray for him" in the summer of 2018. Alone in my car, I looked around to see where it had come from.

More often, though, it is quiet, which is why we must listen closely for it. In fact, the Bible tells us it comes to us in a whisper.

> The LORD said, "Go out and stand on the mountain in the presence of the LORD, for the LORD is about to pass by." Then a great and powerful wind tore the mountains apart and shattered the rocks before the LORD, but the LORD was not in the wind. After the wind there was an earthquake, but the LORD was not in the earthquake. After the earthquake came a fire, but the LORD was not in the fire. And after the fire came a gentle whisper. (1 Kings 19:11–12)

That whisper was God.

How do we know the voice is His? God's message will always line up with Scripture and be consistent with His character, which is another reason to get to know Him through His Word. God will never ask you to do something that is contrary to Scripture.

It isn't that rote prayers don't have a place as a meditative form of prayer. After all, Jesus taught His disciples to pray the Our Father. But rote prayers alone are limiting. If the only conversations I have with a friend or spouse are reading or speaking from a memorized script, how close would I get to them? How well would we know each other without genuine conversation? I could be using all the right words, but would I be having heartfelt talks that encourage and strengthen intimacy? God desires that same intimacy, the kind we seek with a spouse or close friend.

Opening ourselves up to a personal relationship with God requires a form of surrender, trusting God has gone before us, will guide and even orchestrate our life in a way that sometimes might be uncomfortable. *What if God asks me to share my faith at work? What if He wants me to begin a ministry or leave the comfort zone of my job? What if He asks me to do something I've never done before?*

God will use all our experiences for good and growth if we allow it. Three years after my mother's death, seventeen months after the loss of my husband, my sweet grandson went Home. I need look no further than my Facebook Page to a friendship with a man who met Jacob only once, who ten years later claims that meeting my grandson "changed his life." God used even the brief life of a child to touch the life of others, just as He used multiple losses to prepare me for training in grief counseling. He guided me to jobs that would support my three children remaining at home. My first job after David's death was as a library director at a small-town library. During the interview, I was amazed by the board's quick assent to my request to bring my youngest two with me. I never would have had the audacity to propose such an arrangement were it not for the leading of the Holy Spirit in the interview that day.

Only God could lead me to a public speaking ministry despite my lack of verbal skills after years of isolation as a homeschooling mom at home where I'd barely spoken to anyone outside of the butcher and the mailman. He guided me to organize an annual grief retreat even though I knew nothing about running retreats. He blessed me with dozens of Christian friends and mentors and made it possible for me to sign seven book contracts in eight years. Through some difficult and lonely years, God worked in me, and will continue to do so, chipping away at my broken self and wrong attitudes to create a new Mary.

He used nine years of loneliness and spiritual growth to equip me to become the wife that Nick would need three years after he lost his own spouse.

Nick says:

My first wife's death in 2018 forced me to face my own mortality. I wanted to make sure I was headed to heaven. My first step was to add a daily Rosary to my routine. I wasn't sure what I was looking for, but I was seeking something beyond myself, something I'd seen in my brother Pat, who read the Bible daily.

When I met Mary, I was definitely open to praying together. I later learned that if I hadn't readily agreed to pray with her, there wasn't going to be another date, so I'm glad I responded with enthusiasm.

When Mary first asked to pray with me, I admit I was surprised at the prayer. I'd expected either silent prayer or one we'd both memorized as Catholics. Instead, she took hold of my hands and prayed out loud, talking to God as if He was her friend. Husbands, this was so new to me. I remember thinking, *I'll never be able to pray like that.*

When Mary once asked me early on in our dating if I would pray specifically for her, my response was to assure her I would add her to my daily Rosary.

"No," she said. "I need to hear it. I need to hear you talk to God." Up until that moment, she had been the one to pray out loud. I don't remember what I said in that prayer, but I do know it was short and quick. It didn't matter. That was all she needed.

I learned to pray differently after that, eventually in the conversational way Mary used. If I woke up in the middle of the night and couldn't get back to sleep, I'd start talking to God.

I didn't read the Bible right away after we got married, but I was reading devotionals. I wasn't sure how to use the Bible. I think the first verse I ever looked up myself was one I was curious about because I'd seen it on signs at golf courses: "For God so loved the world that he gave his one and only Son, that whoever believes in him shall not perish but have eternal life" (John 3:16).

It took us getting COVID-19 on our first anniversary to get me started reading the Bible. We spent so much time on the couch together, feeling miserable, that we decided to add a video Bible study to our morning ritual. Those studies included readings from the Bible. When I wanted to read more, my brother and Mary suggested I begin with the more easily understood book of Proverbs.

In our second year of marriage, Mary was diagnosed with uterine cancer. My first wife had died from cancer, so naturally, my mind went there. One night, when I had let worry get the best of me, I got up to talk to God. I don't know if this was the first time I heard a response, but it was a clear one. "My son, you will have her for a long time."

The next morning, I told Mary about what I'd heard and asked, "Do you think that was God, or was it just me?"

Mary laughed. "Of course, it was God," she assured me. "You don't call yourself my son." She then reminded me of how I'd immediately been drawn to a painting of her daughter's, snatching it up to purchase before I knew the Bible verse she'd meditated on as she painted it. "My son, give me your heart and let your eyes delight in my ways" (Proverbs 23:26).

"You've given Him your heart, so now He calls you my son," Mary said, before admitting she'd been worried as well, but the answer to my prayer provided reassurance she needed.

The following year, I realized just how powerful prayer could be when I made the decision to sell my business. For thirty-five years, I'd run the business without consulting God, but as soon as I put Him at the forefront of all of it, things were a lot less stressful. It didn't mean everything worked out the way I'd originally hoped or even that the sale went smoothly.

But by asking God what His plans were for the business, I felt the guidance of the Holy Spirit in all of it.

For years, I'd worried about retirement, thinking it was the beginning of the end for most men. Now, knowing God has plans for me, I believe it's just the beginning of discovering His purpose for my life.

DISCUSSION

"And when you pray, do not keep on babbling like pagans, for they think they will be heard because of their many words. Do not be like them, for your Father knows what you need before you ask him."

MATTHEW 6:7–8

1. What is your background regarding your prayer habits? What did you learn about prayer from your parents? Have you ever seen a couple praying together?

2. What is your relationship with God like? What was it like when you were a child? Does it feel like a personal relationship?

   Note: If this is the first time you've considered what it means to have a personal relationship with God, don't get discouraged. We all have a starting place in our commitment to Christ. Mary was fifty-two, and Nick was sixty-eight when they reached that point. Our Creator welcomes this relationship at whatever point you are.

3. Neither Nick nor Mary read the Bible before they began seeking a personal relationship with God, but it has become integral to their faith. Do you read the Bible? If not, why not? How could you get started?

4. Matthew 6:7–8 makes it clear that your prayers don't have to be fancy or full of important words. There is no right or wrong way to pray if it comes from the heart. God prefers genuine, heartfelt prayers from His children. If you don't already pray with your spouse, what do you think is holding you back?

Hold hands as you read this prayer out loud together:

Lord, God, we welcome You into our relationship. We want You to be the cord that binds us together. We ask You to work in our lives. Help us build up our marriage to be the union You intend it to be. Guide us as we discover the purpose and plan You have for us and in our prayer life.

Chapter 3

Second Act

Therefore, if anyone is in Christ, the new creation has come: The old has gone, the new is here!

2 CORINTHIANS 5:17

Mary:

"Don't you think the reason your marriage is so good is because of your age and all you have been through?" a friend asked.

"Well, of course, this relationship is different than what you experienced before. You two aren't raising children together," another said.

We've fielded comments like these ever since we began publicly sharing how extraordinary our marriage relationship is, something we attribute to God and, more specifically, our practice of praying together. While there is certainly some truth to such statements, they also tend to minimize what it means to have a marriage relationship centered on God as the third cord that binds a couple.

The Bible describes it this way:

> Two are better than one, because they have a good return for their labor: If either of them falls down, one can help the other up. But pity anyone who falls and has no one to help them up. Also, if two lie down together, they will keep warm. But how can one keep warm alone? Though one may be overpowered, two can defend themselves. A cord of three strands is not quickly broken. (Ecclesiastes 4:9–12)

By inviting God into our relationship from our second date, Nick and I committed to including Him in every aspect of our union, a partnership of three. Praying together unites us spiritually, strengthening the bond between us and God.

We are both convinced praying together would have benefited our first marriages. How could it not? Praying together is one of the most intimate things a couple can do together. By the world's standards, we had perfectly good marriages. We loved our previous spouses. Grieved the loss of them. Could we have had with our previous partner what we have now with each other? Well, yes, and no.

The answer is not as simple as our age or family situation. Hindsight and personal growth in our faith allow us to look back at our first marriages and see what was clearly missing, not because of fault or flaw in our marriage partner, but because of who *we* were. Simply put, neither one of us is the same person we were in our first marriages. I am not the woman who was married to David. Nick is not the man who was married to Mindy. During our first marriages, we did not know God in a personal way or put Him at the center of those relationships.

Jesus said to His disciples, "I am the way and the truth and the life. No one comes to the Father except through me. If you really know me, you will know my Father as well" (John 14:6–7). Until we accepted Jesus as our Savior and read His Word to get to know Him, we could not experience the kind of marriage we have now, one that includes God in the partnership. We were inwardly changed through our personal relationship with Jesus.

This truth is critical to understanding the difference in our second marriage. We look back, and our life with our previous spouses feels separate from the God-centered life we live now. Because it is. That's an uncomfortable admission because both of us wish, for the sake of those first spouses, that we had been the person we are now while we were married to them.

One of the cornerstones of the Christian faith is that once a person accepts Christ and makes the decision to follow Him, they become a new person, with Christ residing in them in the form of the Holy Spirit. That indwelling of the Holy Spirit *demands* a change from our former way of living.

I made the conscious decision to turn to God in 2012. My mother's death in 2010 opened the door, but it took the death of a husband for me to walk through it and actively seek God. I didn't fully realize at the time that through my choice, I was given the gift of the Holy Spirit. But that's what the Bible promises, a promise we will discuss more in a later chapter.

I did have an inkling God was actively working in my life to refine me, to make me a better person, more like Jesus. During the darkest period of my life, I was being drawn closer to God, sensing His nearness. I could see His light in the people He brought into my life, mentors who encouraged me in faith.

While the changes in me might not have looked dramatic on the surface, there was no doubt God was refining me, working in and through me in big and small ways, creating the Mary He'd always meant me to be—a woman who prays continually, one who turns to her Bible for wisdom and guidance and has learned to discern His voice, a woman who continues to grow in trust and faith. God brought me to a place where I would listen to an unseen voice in 2018 and obey, praying for the stranger that He promised would become her husband.

I remember the first time I realized I'd become an entirely different person, someone transformed. It was in June 2012, just a couple of months after David died. I'd won a Cecil Murphey scholarship to a Christian writing conference in Wheaton, Illinois. The very last book David had held in his hands was Don Piper and Cecil Murphey's *Getting to Heaven.*[1] The conference would end on what would have been our anniversary. I was awarded the scholarship on the evening of my husband's wake. All signs pointed to God's orchestration.

Much of that conference is a blur except for a few powerful moments; the conference turned out to be an extremely spiritual experience for me. It was on the final day when I realized I was no longer the same Mary, the isolated homeschooling mother of eight who didn't trust many people, especially women. Females had been my worst tormentors in grade school, had stabbed me in the back in high school. Outside of my sisters, I'd had only one female friend as an adult and convinced myself one was all I needed.

Looking back, I believe God began opening my eyes and preparing me for the loss of a spouse the previous year when I attended my first Christian writer's conference, which was where I'd observed the example of Christian women who prayed in a way I'd never heard before, personalized prayer from the heart.

I heard that kind of praying again in Wheaton. Sitting around the breakfast table the final morning, on the day that would have been my anniversary, I was surrounded by a group of women I didn't know. They were talking and laughing animatedly. I sat silently bereft, grief thrusting me on the outskirts just as I had so often been in my years of grade school, high school, and as a homeschooling mother, an outsider.

The conversation turned serious. Someone asked for prayers for her roommate, who'd fallen that morning. I looked up, glancing around the table as the women took hold of each other's hands to pray for a stranger. I bowed my head as the woman next to me grasped my hand in hers, warming me with the camaraderie of the impromptu group I now belonged to. I truly felt I belonged to God's family, one of his daughters.

I love these women. That stark realization hit me with a jolt. Who was I, seeing other women that way, this species I could never seem to trust? *I love them.* My eyes darted from one to another: young, old, women of all sizes and shapes. I nearly gasped out loud. *These women praying together? They are beautiful.*

I was seeing the cluster of women through God's eyes. I most definitely was not the same Mary. Remarkably, I would someday become the kind of woman who would obey the Holy Spirit's prompting to approach a stranger and ask if I could pray for him, something I would never have done just ten years before.

I did just that recently in the waiting room of the VA hospital as Nick had his blood drawn. An older man across the room grimaced as he adjusted something attached to his abdomen beneath his shirt. His eyes met mine, and I caught a glimpse of pain before he leaned over, head down, shoulders slumped. Something told me he urgently needed prayer, and I was to deliver it.

I hesitated only briefly before approaching him.

"Can I pray for you?" I asked. He nodded in assent, and tears streamed down his face as I touched his shoulder and prayed out loud. God had, indeed, refined me. I'd become the kind of woman God could use to bring comfort to a hurting stranger.

Nick says:

Someone recently commented that they envied my transformation story. They'd accepted Jesus as their Savior when they were a child and had been following Him ever since, and here I'd experienced this dramatic change in my life as an adult.

When I consider my journey of faith, I think about the quiet alone time I had during those last ten weeks when my first wife, Mindy, was in hospice. She often slept when I visited, so I'd go to the cafeteria or the chapel by myself. It was in that solitude I'd think about death and dying, natural in that setting, when I'd seen several other patients die. I believe now God was reaching out to me, but it wasn't until Mindy died that I really searched my soul. Where would I end up when I died? What could I do to ensure it would be heaven?

After Mindy's death, my cousin Nancy sent me a set of four books called *Journeying Through Grief*.[2] I wasn't much of a reader, but the books were easy to read and included a lot of biblical insight regarding grief. Those books and my morning ritual of praying the Rosary opened me up to thinking more about God and heaven.

I wish I'd had the support system Mary had. I remember a lot of months of anxiety and confusion trying to figure out things myself. I wasn't always making the best decisions. I had no clear direction in my life. I did turn to my brother Pat and my sister Mary Kay because it seemed as if they had answers I didn't. I'd noticed my brother Pat always read the Bible, even on vacation, and that intrigued me too. I'd never read the Bible. But that curiosity still didn't make me begin reading it.

Something about Mary's dating profile appealed to me. She made it clear she was looking for a man of faith and that the Bible was part of her life. I was truthful when I told her I was seeking whatever it was that she and my brother had. Still, before that first meeting, I worried I might be too "rough around the edges" for someone like her and told her so.

I'd owned a business for over thirty years, one that I described as a bowling center/banquet hall in my messages to Mary, but it also included a bar. It wasn't until I started dating Mary and following God that I became aware of the negative aspects of the drinking and barroom talk I'd surrounded myself with. I realized that in attempting to protect her from some of it, I wasn't enjoying the atmosphere so much myself anymore. I was looking at everything differently, through the eyes of my future wife and, more importantly, God's eyes, and I came up short. I didn't want to be that man anymore.

It wasn't an overnight change. I didn't kneel and say a prayer and instantly become a new man, like our friend seemed to think when she expressed envy about my transformation. But I look back now and think about that first date with Mary in a different way. She had a Bible verse on her wall that I asked her about. I also asked her how she got started reading the Bible. She explained what it meant to her to have a personal relationship with God and sent me home with a Max Lucado daily devotional and her book *Refined by Fire: A Journey of Grief and Grace,*[3] which I read in two nights—unheard of for me.

Was that the turning point for me, or was it with the next date, when Mary took my hands in hers and prayed for me personally and for us as a couple? Because as soon as I began dating Mary, I watched my language, prayed with her, and began reading devotionals. And though I didn't begin reading it immediately, one of her wedding gifts to me was a leather-bound Max Lucado Bible.

Instinctively, I knew to distance myself from my former life after Mary and I got married. A couple of years later, I watched Phil Robertson's faith story in *The Blind* movie and noticed he'd done the same thing when he started following Jesus, moving away from the environment that had encouraged his bad behavior.

Semi-retired, I sold my house and moved back to the hometown where I'd grown up, where Mary worked. We'd work together at the bowling center sometimes, but my grandson took over the bulk of the management. I sold the business two years later and never looked back. I no longer find my identity in owning a business but in whatever God has in store for me for these last years of my life.

I am doing things I would never have imagined doing: co-coordinating an annual writer's conference, public speaking with Mary, and co-writing this book. Anyone who knew me in high school would laugh at the idea of me working on a book, which should be proof enough that God can change someone if He can change someone like me.

DISCUSSION

Do not lie to each other, since you have taken off your old self with its practices and have put on the new self, which is being renewed in knowledge in the image of its Creator.

Colossians 3: 9–10

1. Can you recall a point in your life you decided to follow Jesus? Was it more of a gradual process? Share your "before" and "after" faith story with your spouse. If you haven't made this decision, how would you describe your current understanding of faith?

2. Both Mary and Nick attended church with their families but didn't comprehend that eternal salvation requires more than believing in God and going to church. Even Satan believes in God. The Bible says, "You believe that there is one God. Good! Even the demons believe that—and shudder" (James 2:19). What were you taught about getting to heaven?

3. As you step out in faith as a couple to deepen your prayer life, you will want to protect your marriage from the inevitable attacks from the Evil One. Read the following verses together.

Finally, be strong in the Lord and in his mighty power. Put on the full armor of God, so that you can take your stand against the devil's schemes. For our struggle is not against flesh and blood, but against the rulers, against the authorities, against the powers of this dark world and against the spiritual forces of evil in the heavenly realms. Therefore, put on the full armor of God, so that when the day of evil comes, you may be able to stand your ground, and after you have done everything, to stand. Stand firm then, with the belt of truth buckled around your waist, with the breastplate of righteousness in place, and with your feet fitted with the readiness that comes from the gospel of peace. In addition to all this, take up the shield of faith, with which you can extinguish all the flaming arrows of the evil one. Take the helmet of salvation and the sword of the Spirit, which is the word of God.

Ephesians 6:10–17

Chapter 4

Flaming Arrows

Be alert and of sober mind. Your enemy the devil prowls around like a roaring lion looking for someone to devour. Resist him, standing firm in the faith, because you know that the family of believers throughout the world is undergoing the same kind of sufferings.

1 PETER 5:8–9

Mary:

When a friend suggested that Nick and I begin each day reading the Ephesians armor of God section of the Bible, I pulled out the well-worn copy of those same verses I'd carried in my purse for ten years, ever since a particularly stressful time in my life when I'd felt as though I was being spiritually attacked.

The topic of Satan is not a pleasant subject, one I managed to avoid for most of my adult life. But once I made the conscious decision to follow Jesus, the dark forces of evil were revealed to me in a myriad of ways. This is another truth I discovered very early on in my relationship with Nick and one I wished I'd been aware of in my previous marriage. There is nothing Satan would like better than to infiltrate a marriage.

The Bible warns that Satan is a master of deception and lies. "You belong to your father, the devil, and you want to carry out your father's desires. He was a murderer from the beginning, not holding to the truth, for there is no truth in him. When he lies, he speaks his native language, for he is a liar and the father of lies" (John 8:44).

The devil's schemes are deceptive, his strongholds elusive, but the closer we get to God, the easier it is to recognize the devil's work. During the darkest times in my life, I experienced encounters I can now see clearly as the spiritual warfare the Bible teaches us to be prepared for.

A spiritual mentor once explained to me that until the night my mother died in 2010, I had lived a life neither so good nor so bad that I'd drawn the attention of the devil. It was my mother's example and legacy of faith that started me down my own path of faith, my journey inevitably drawing the attention of the Evil One, whose goal is to "steal and kill and destroy" (John 10:10). Satan wants to rob us of eternal life.

Though I'd never thought about Satan much as an adult, I certainly did as a child. Not only did I read an entire children's Bible the summer between third and fourth grade, but I was also the little girl who'd sit in the pasture waiting for Jesus or Mary to appear. I was a natural-born daydreamer, entertained by my own imagination. Words and images were important for an avid reader, budding artist, and writer. I held elaborate conversations in my head as I walked eight blocks to my Catholic school, where I learned in religion class that words or images could be sinful. So, it was with some consternation I found myself struggling to fall asleep when a curse word I'd heard or an image I'd seen wouldn't leave my thoughts.

"Please, God, take it away," I'd pray as I tossed and turned, sleep eluding me. It didn't help that my mother's nighttime prayer ritual included the lines "if I should die before I wake." Once she left the room, I'd lie in the dark wondering just why a ten-year-old might die in the night or worse, if my parents might die while I slept. An overactive imagination, perhaps, but one that would serve me well in later years when I began writing for publication.

Was it irony or a strategic move that Satan would use that same childhood weakness against me as an adult some fifty years later? The woman who had been plagued as a child by "bad" words and images, who never said a swear word in her life, would marry a man who had been surrounded by coarseness in his work environment. Though he was careful with his language after he met me, there was the rare slip-up that gave me a glimpse of the old Nick. Comments from those who knew him before his commitment to Christ reinforced the idea that Nick had been a product of his environment.

Once, in the early days of our marriage, Nick made the mistake of sharing a joke he used to tell younger men when he beat their bowling scores. I was shocked by the crassness of it, further appalled when he didn't immediately show regret. He apologized before he left for work, but I couldn't get his gaffe out of my head. That was not the Nick I knew and loved. Satan had found a stronghold. What better way to mess with Mary than get into her head and plant seeds of doubt about her husband and his past. *Did he really change? Was he truly a new man? Does he miss that old life?* Or worse, *Can I trust his love for me? His love for God?* The crude words reverberated in my head for most of the morning until I called my daughter Emily to ask for prayer.

"Grace and mercy, Mom," she gently rebuked, reminding me of this Scripture verse: "But he gives us more grace. That is why Scripture says: 'God opposes the proud but shows favor to the humble'" (James 4:6).

I needed to give Nick mercy. Neither one of us was perfect. Only with God's grace could either of us live a victorious Christian life.

It didn't help my personal struggle with Nick's past that he had his own weakness in not articulating his thoughts or feelings well, only adding to my angst. I'd hear something he hadn't meant, his remark playing a loop in my head, growing more and more insidious, feeding my insecurities. Six hours after an innocuous comment on his part, I'd question him. "When you said this morning that when you met me, you cared more about the inner person than the outer, did that mean you didn't find me attractive?"

He'd look at me, shaking his head impatiently at my incredulous way of thinking, which only served to worsen my anxiety. I couldn't bear his irritation aimed at me. To his credit, he never got angry, but he was frustrated, not sure how to respond. It didn't make sense to either of us that reminders of Nick's past could prompt a reel to play in my head. He hadn't even been married to me then. He wasn't the Nick I knew and loved.

Recognizing it for what it was—spiritual warfare—we knew we needed to "armor up" with the tools of truth, righteousness, knowledge of God's Word, and most of all, prayer. As for me, I had to learn to take my thoughts captive whenever the reels started. It helped to imagine God's hand grasping the thoughts in my head and throwing them away. Nick responded in a similar manner when he recognized my loop of "stinking thinking." He'd flatten his palm against my forehead, then swiftly pull it away, a gesture that meant, "Get Satan out of your head."

It's interesting to note how God used the very workplace environment that continually reminded me of my husband's past to do His work in me. Nick was proud of the business he'd built up, one that supported his family well in the thirty-three years he'd run it. Early in our dating days, he gave me a tour of the building, beginning in the banquet hall where events such as funeral luncheons, wedding receptions, and private parties were held. The tour moved to the kitchen, then his office, followed by the bright and colorful bowling area. It ended in the lounge area, where meals were served. I studiously avoided looking at the bar area, uncomfortable with the environment.

A few months after we were married, God made it clear He wanted me to leave my well-paying job. I struggled with the decision. It didn't make sense. I was good at my job and loved talking about faith every day. Still, I obeyed, assuming God must have something incredibly exciting in store for me—maybe writing a new book or doing more public speaking. Nick dropped most of his own hours, thrilled to have more time with me and looking forward to the possibility of traveling together.

Shortly after my resignation, Nick got a call from a longtime employee. Her husband was dying of cancer, and she wanted to be home with him. We offered to take over her hours. For the next several weeks, I worked at Nick's side, cleaning, serving funeral lunches, and waitressing while he cooked, made drinks, and manned the register.

I remember one particularly busy day covering the lunch crowd. Exhausted by rushing from table to table and taking orders, I perched on a stool to take a break. Leaning on the counter, I took a deep breath and looked around, studying the surroundings.

Really? I left my job for this; to clean and serve others, working for tips? I couldn't understand it. Why would God have me leave a good-paying job where I could share my faith and pray with coworkers to volunteer as a waitress? My distaste for the bar area had diminished somewhat by then, though I would never be completely comfortable in it.

When we first started working together, Nick inevitably got an earful on the way home as I criticized patrons who spent half their afternoon drinking at the bar. "What a waste of a life," I'd comment, expecting him to agree with me. Instead, he'd gently admonish me, correctly pointing out I had no idea what their life was like. I soon realized his compassionate viewpoint was much more Christlike than my judgmental one.

My rumination at the counter continued. *Had God brought me to this place so He could work in me to be less judgmental?* I considered the very real possibility. Then I pondered how good it was for me to see Nick's prowess in his old environment, how fun it was to watch him cook and interact with regular patrons, even though I knew I wasn't seeing the old Nick. Regular patrons often commented on the difference in him. *Was that another reason we'd been brought here? So Nick could demonstrate he was a changed man?*

My reverie was interrupted as a plate of food was placed in front of me. I turned to see the broad smile on my husband's face. Everything I needed to know was right there, reflected in his eyes. *Gratitude. Companionship. Love. So much love.*

God, in His infinite wisdom, had brought us together. Nick was exactly who I needed. The smoothing and polishing of his previous rough edges attested to his transformation. God took a man who had been of the world and transformed him into one of faith, a man who would help me grow in Christian maturity. Nick had truly become a son of our ultimate Father, and a father figure to my children and their spouses, an example of faith to my grandchildren.

God knew exactly what He was doing when He led me to leave my job. He knew Nick would be called back to work.

He perceived that my ability to see regular customers through Nick's eyes would humanize them and humble me. Most importantly, God had a purpose and a plan for us as a couple. Those weeks of working side by side prepared us to take over co-coordinating an annual Christian writer's conference and for what came next.

God delights in surprises. That book writing and public speaking I thought He might have in store for me? Turned out, team Nick and Mary would be speaking together on the power of prayer and co-writing a book on the same topic.

More than we could have imagined or asked for.

Nick says:

Like Mary, I didn't think about Satan much for most of my life. I knew he existed, but I never considered he might have influenced my life in any way. I always considered myself a pretty good guy compared to a lot of men I knew. I did more good than bad, so I thought it would even out in the end, like if I went to church on Sunday and said a couple memorized prayers each night, I would be okay. I can look back and see how wrong I was. It upsets me now that I didn't see the sinfulness in my life.

I have regrets. Who doesn't? I regret volunteering to join the Army when I was barely seventeen because that probably hardened me in some ways. Mary says I am a huge influence on her children and grandchildren, and though I appreciate that (and feel honored by it), it makes me have regrets about the kind of father I was to my own children. Owning a business,

I worked seven days a week to give my children vacations and material items when I should have spent more time with them. I'm sure I failed them in other ways I don't even know about. I can't do anything about past mistakes or go back and change things. I did what I thought was best at the time. Regrets don't change anything, and God doesn't want me to hold onto them.

I had a hard time understanding the stronghold Satan had over Mary's thoughts at first, and for a long time was convinced I didn't have any strongholds of my own. Maybe that was part of the problem, my inability to recognize any weakness in myself. My pride got in the way, especially early on in our marriage. I often got defensive about choices I'd made in the past, not wanting to admit I'd ever made mistakes, partly because I wasn't sure God could forgive me, even though deep down inside, I know He had.

Mary has a strong sense of right and wrong. That's what attracted me to her in the first place, but I didn't always like it when she'd make a valid point about morality or values, even if I knew she was right. Especially if she was right. It wasn't until recently that I realized my enjoyment of proving someone else wrong could be a foothold Satan would use against our marriage, my defensiveness planting seeds of doubt in my wife's head.

I still think the devil likes to mess with Mary more than he does with me, at least regarding the "stinking thinking" she talks about. It's easier for me to take control of my thoughts than it is for her. I can talk to God, and negative thinking usually goes away.

But with Mary, it might take hours before something I said bothers her. I sometimes see it happening to her before she does. I'll even say, "Go pray," to remind her she has God's power to help her. We both do.

The truth is, neither one of us can excuse our old behaviors with statements like "I'm just not patient," "I can't control my thoughts," or "I'm just not good with words." Not anymore, because now we know better. Our old self is gone. God has changed us and will continue to change us. I couldn't have written these words during our first year of marriage when my pride still had such a hold on me, but thanks to the work of the Holy Spirit in me, I can now.

DISCUSSION

Submit yourselves, then, to God. Resist the devil, and he will flee from you. Come near to God and he will come near to you.

James 4:7–8

1. What weakness in you might give Satan a foothold in your everyday life? How can you, as a couple, address those potential pitfalls?

2. Like Nick could see the devil messing with Mary, do you see an area where your spouse might be vulnerable to the Enemy?

3. Luke 6:36 tells us, "Be merciful, just as your Father is merciful." Mary's daughter admonished her to give Nick mercy and grace when he stumbled in his faith journey. How can you practice mercy and grace with your spouse?

4. Are you spending time with God daily? If not, why do you think that is? What one thing can you begin doing today that will allow you to spend more time in prayer or reading. What changes would you need to make in your lifestyle?

Use this space to write down a prayer for your spouse. Read your prayers out loud to each other.

His

Hers

Chapter 5

The Pruning

"He cuts off every branch in me that bears no fruit, while every branch that does bear fruit he prunes so that it will be even more fruitful."

John 15:2

Mary:

Two years into our marriage, I had an epiphany as Nick and I did a Bible study on Galatians.

> The acts of the flesh are obvious: sexual immorality, impurity and debauchery; idolatry and witchcraft; hatred, discord, jealousy, fits of rage, selfish ambition, dissensions, factions and envy; drunkenness, orgies, and the like. I warn you, as I did before, that those who live like this will not inherit the kingdom of God. (Galatians 5:19–21)

It had been easy for me to identify sins in Nick's past. The changes in his life after he began following Jesus seemed dramatic compared to mine. I'd often ponder the Bible verse that says, "I tell you that in the same way there will be more rejoicing in heaven over one sinner who repents than over ninety-nine righteous persons who do not need to repent" (Luke 15:7). I imagined there had been more rejoicing in heaven over Nick's coming to Christ than when I had.

Evidently, I was under the impression I was more righteous and needed less repentance than my husband, which was a sinful attitude. What a shock it was when it dawned on me just how many of those acts of flesh identified in Galatians 5:19 I had been guilty of before developing a personal relationship with God. *Discord. Jealousy. Selfish ambition. Dissension. Faction. Envy.* Add *delight in gossip* to that roster of sins. It had been so much easier to identify the "speck in someone else's eye than the log in my own" (Matthew 7:3–5, paraphrased).

Let me tell you a story about a counselor, a social worker, and a nun . . .

It sounds like the beginning of a bad joke, but there was nothing funny about seeking help in my first marriage. I'd had glimpses of David's quick temper during our dating days. When I stood in front of the priest in 1979 at the age of nineteen to proclaim our marriage vows, I had no idea my husband's anger would intensify to the point of "fits of rage" that would eventually send us to marriage counseling. I was convinced David was the problem, not me. His anger was unreasonable, unlike my response, which seemed perfectly reasonable considering the emotional pain he inflicted.

In hindsight, I see how I contributed to the unhealthy patterns we developed as a couple, particularly with my inability to see David as the head of our household. *Because I didn't think a man who couldn't control his anger deserved respect.* I couldn't trust his temper, so I couldn't trust him. My disdain for his volatile temper resulted in a lack of respect for him, a lack he most surely felt. That lack of respect did not help our relationship.

We were nearly fourteen years into our marriage before we sought help from a social worker through Catholic Charities. An older version of my husband, the man had also raised a large family on a low income. Being able to vent to someone who understood that lifestyle seemed to help, but David's simmering anger remained. Later, it was free counseling services offered at a local hospital, but that counselor seemed to have more troubles than we did. He was divorced, and his oldest son had recently attempted suicide. Eventually, our priest recommended a nun trained in counseling. We saw her for two years. She was the first one to suggest my husband's upbringing, or lack thereof, might have something to do with his anger, along with the car accident and subsequent coma he'd been in as a teen. While that was valuable insight for both of us, it didn't solve our underlying problem.

None of these counselors suggested we pray together or seek answers from the Bible, not even the two who came from a faith-based perspective. Why didn't they?

Ultimately, it would be David's bout with cancer and my subsequent caregiving stint in 2006 that served to break some of the old patterns. Despite the wake-up call, we still didn't turn to God together, though I believe now David did, independently of me, in the last year of his life. What would our relationship have looked like if we'd included God in it beyond that moment at the altar? How could our lives have been different if we'd read and studied the Bible together, prayerfully discerning God's will in our lives? What would it have meant for our children to see a marriage relationship like that?

What if just one of those counselors had suggested we follow the Ephesians design for marriage?

> Submit to one another out of reverence for Christ. Wives, submit yourselves to your own husbands as you do to the Lord. For the husband is the head of the wife as Christ is the head of the church, his body, of which he is the Savior . . . In this same way, husbands ought to love their wives as their own bodies. He who loves his wife

> loves himself. . . . each one of you also must love his wife as he loves himself, and the wife must respect her husband. (Ephesians 5:21–23, 28, 33)

Would we have listened, taken the words to heart, and followed them? I'll never know. What I do know is that after ten years of pursuing a personal relationship with God, I was convinced even before I met Nick that God would need to be the third party in any future romance. The partnership would entail three: husband, wife, and God. I was eager to demonstrate I could be an Ephesians 5 kind of wife.

God had already done a lot of pruning in me during the ten years I was single. Widowed at fifty-two, four children still at home, I turned to Him in desperation, clinging to Jeremiah 29:11 like it was a bungee cord to God and a personal promise. "'For I know the plans I have for you,' declares the Lord, 'plans to prosper you and not to harm you, plans to give you hope and a future.'"

God did have a future planned for me—one I could never have imagined. I became a different person, not despite grief, but because of it. God guided me to the right jobs, Christian mentors, and a ministry in speaking and writing. He brought me the husband He'd asked me to pray for three years before. I had to learn to align my priorities with God's will, to trust and submit to Him, trust and submit to a husband as well.

The word *submit* has gotten a bad rap. I once spoke with a young woman about how an adjustment in her attitude could make life easier for her boyfriend. She later told someone I'd advised her to become a doormat, and she refused to be that for any man. I'd meant just the opposite. Women are extremely powerful serving as the helper described in the Bible: "The LORD God said, 'It is not good for man to be alone. I will make a helper suitable for him'" (Genesis 2:18).

By the time I met Nick, I thought I had it all figured out: the wifely submission, the rightful place of the man at the head of a household, the whole Proverbs 31 womanly ideal. It didn't take too long after our wedding day for me to realize God had work to do in me yet. I needed to abandon the self-righteous attitude and face my own sins. I'm still growing in my faith and likely will be until the day I die.

One way God continues to work in me is through the way I treat my husband. Treasuring Nick as the gift that he is, I can serve him in the same way Jesus served His disciples when He washed their feet. Nick need never doubt he is cherished by me.

Want to be a treasure in your husband's eyes? I guarantee you will be when you take the time to demonstrate your love for him in tangible ways. When Nick recently told his doctor that I rubbed his feet daily to help with neuropathy, she wryly commented, "My husband would love that. He even asks for it sometimes after work, but I'm just too tired."

Wives, it takes ten minutes to rub your husband's feet. Or their shoulders if you can't stand to touch feet. Ten minutes. It doesn't have to be a foot or shoulder rub. There are other ways to show your husband how much you treasure him. I promise you will never regret those few minutes.

Nick says:

"I bet Mary won't let you." I remember the first time I heard those words and how much they bothered me. I'd always done pretty much whatever I wanted to do, and when I started to change, people who knew me before took notice, assuming the changes in me were because of Mary, and I didn't like that. The truth is, Mary's faith did influence me, but it was God who was changing me.

I had a stubborn will to deal with. I didn't like to admit parts of my past had been sinful, and I certainly didn't want anyone telling me what to do. I still hate to admit I'm wrong and sometimes joke, "I thought I was wrong once, but I was mistaken."

I also knew not everyone would believe, understand, or welcome the changes in me, like the person who recently commented about the difference in me, "Well, I sure hope Mary hasn't changed your sense of humor."

Mary didn't change anything, but God did. I'll always have a sense of humor. It's been part of me since I was a kid. It's how I learned to deal with things. But I had over thirty-five years of material from a bar atmosphere that I knew I couldn't, or shouldn't, share with my new wife. When we were first married, I'd still occasionally pull a guy aside to share one of my old jokes, until that felt uncomfortable too. The change happened gradually. The closer I got to God, the less I enjoyed the kinds of jokes I shielded my wife from, realizing I needed new material. The Bible makes it pretty clear how we should talk. "Above all else, guard your heart, for everything you do flows from it. Keep your mouth free of perversity; keep corrupt talk far from your lips" (Proverbs 4:23–24).

It's not a bad thing that what amuses me has changed. Now, I can find enjoyment in watching a Christian comedian like Tim Hawkins or telling "dad jokes." Mary always laughs at my corny jokes. In fact, we laugh all the time. We laugh in the car. We even start laughing over something in the middle of the night! We've been known to hold back a chuckle in church. I love making people laugh, especially Mary. That's not going to change. I'm convinced God has a sense of humor.

I didn't know Mary had prayed for me before our first public speaking engagement together. Evidently, she'd asked God to give me a chance to use my sense of humor because she knew that would make me more comfortable the next time we spoke together. The topic was serious—praying together as a couple—so, for most of it, I didn't get that chance. When someone asked a question after our presentation, Mary didn't know I'd already turned off the microphone. When it didn't work, she glanced at me.

"You turned me off," she accused.

"If only it were that easy," I quipped back, and the room erupted in laughter.

I worried about my response as we walked back to the car. Had I hurt her feelings? Instead, when we got into the car, she immediately started laughing.

"I can't believe you said that! It was perfect! It had to be God because the words out of my mouth set you up perfectly. Normally, I would have said, 'You turned it off,' but instead, I said, 'You turned *me* off!' I'd asked God to give you the opportunity to use your humor, and he sure did."

Even my temperament has changed. When Mary and I were first dating, if I'd get upset with an "idiot driver" on the road or someone's bad parking job in a store lot, I'd loudly proclaim my irritation. Mary offered a different perspective, commenting, "Maybe their spouse just died," or "What if they were just diagnosed with cancer and didn't have their mind on their parking?" That irritated me a little until I realized her perspective was the better one. I'm only partly joking when I admit I hate it when she is right!

I look at a lot of things differently since I started to follow Jesus. God is changing me, but like my wife, I'm still a work in progress. The biggest difference in my new life is that instead of living for myself, I'm living for God, asking Him to guide my choices and decisions. And that's a good change.

DISCUSSION

"Search me, God, and know my heart;
test me and know my anxious thoughts.
See if there is any offensive way in me
and lead me in the way everlasting."

Psalm 139:23–24

1. Mary admits she had a difficult time submitting to and respecting her first husband. As a new Christian, Nick struggled to submit his will to God's authority. Do you struggle when it comes to submission in your relationship with your spouse or God? If so, how?

2. When you read the entire section of Ephesians, note that the passage begins with talking about submitting to one another. What do you think it means to mutually submit to one another?

3. Husbands, Scripture admonishes you to love your wife and treat her like you would your own body. What does that mean to you?

4. Search your heart. Is there something in your life, an attitude or action preventing you from becoming more like Jesus and fulfilling God's purpose and plan for you?

Pray this prayer together:

Lord Jesus, we invite You into our life. Search our hearts for anything that comes between us and You and any attitudes that hinder our devotion to You. Help us become more like Christ. We invite You into our marriage relationship. We want our relationship to always reflect You.

Chapter 6

Sticks and Stones

Gracious words are a honeycomb, sweet to the soul and healing to the bones.

Proverbs 16:24

Mary:

Words, written or spoken, have always been important to me, even as a child. As soon as I learned to read at the age of five, I became a regular patron of our small-town library. Initially, books were simply a form of entertainment. When I began attending a Catholic elementary school, they became a form of escape from the reality of the bullying I encountered there. I wrote my first book at the age of ten, a primitively illustrated tome of prose and poetry I discovered in my mother's things after her death. Had she saved it because she'd seen a potential author in me? Was that why she'd snuck a Big Chief tablet and a pack of number two pencils in my underwear drawer when I was in sixth grade? Because it was this kind of encouragement that led me to believe I could be a writer someday.

I always treasured words of encouragement, saving notes my teachers wrote to my parents, even the one that informed them I was a daydreamer, a description I was secretly proud of. *Daydreamer* sounded so creative.

My dad's handwriting was especially dear to me, considering he wasn't a demonstrative man and rarely expressed his feelings. I'd snatch his notes from the table, instructions for me and my brothers regarding the chores we were assigned to complete before he and Mom arrived home from the store or a doctor's appointment.

"Mary, put the potatoes on," one note said. A saved birthday card is inscribed, "Happy birthday a day late and a dollar short." There's also a white gift box I saved because he'd written on the lid, "Happy birthday, Mary, one day late, Father." Fifty years have passed, and I still cherish these pieces of memorabilia, along with the few letters Dad wrote to me after I left for college in 1978.

In 2009, a year before she died, my mother gave me a real treasure in the box of letters she'd written to her mother in the sixties, giving me a glimpse into the life of the young mother she was as she raised ten children. I organized those letters in two leather binders and filled another two with the letters Mom had written me, along with some of my return ones. Through them, my youngest can see how eagerly I awaited her arrival, just as excited as I was about the impending birth of my first baby.

With this background, it's no surprise I wrote letters and sent cards to Nick even before we were married. I assumed he would reciprocate in a similar manner, with written words of love. It wasn't long before those high expectations crashed with reality.

The reality was, though Nick and his previous wife had exchanged greeting cards for anniversaries and Valentine's Day, neither one had added more than a simple signature, and from the cards I discovered when we packed Nick's things for our first move, it appeared Mindy often signed hers with just the letter "M." How could a man with that background possibly understand or meet my expectation of love notes? The answer was he couldn't unless I managed to explain how important they were to me.

Which I did. Repeatedly. We were dating when I first asked him to write down the words "Everything will be okay" so I could tape the note to my desk at work. To his credit, Nick did seem to understand that a woman who'd reached over to wake her husband up one day, only to find he'd died sometime during the night, might have some abandonment issues and worry about something happening to him too.

Bless his heart, Nick didn't hesitate. He wrote the very words of assurance I needed, then signed the note NJP before handing it to me. I took one look and handed it right back to him. "Nope, you're not going to get away with that with me," I informed him. "You have to sign it personally, with your first name."

I don't think Nick believed me when we faced our first Christmas together and I informed him the best gift I could receive would be his written words, but it was true. He was aware of my subterfuge in choosing the "perfect" gift for him, so he likely couldn't imagine how a gift of mere words could compete with that lengthy search. But they weren't mere words to me. Knowing how difficult it was for Nick to articulate feelings and emotions, for him to take the time to convey them in writing would mean more than any material gift ever could.

For a woman who claims power in words, I look back and am ashamed to admit there were occasions when I intentionally used my verbal skills to hurt David, excusing my behavior with the adage "hurt people hurt people." His diagnosis of oral cancer in 2006 prompted a dramatic change in our relationship. I can't say if his irrational anger disappeared with the cancer treatment or with my caregiving, but for those last five years of his life, he was even-tempered, and my words and actions were kinder and gentler in response.

Once I began studying the Bible, I could no longer rationalize or excuse some of my previous behavior as a spouse. I knew if I ever fell in love again, I wanted to be the biblical wife described in Proverbs. I repeatedly read the book of Proverbs, underlining verses like "A gentle answer turns away wrath, but a harsh word stirs up anger" (v. 15:1) and "She speaks with wisdom, and faithful instruction is on her tongue" (v. 31:26).

When my friend Susan heard I was marrying a man I'd known less than six weeks, she'd worried. "I've known you three years, and I don't really know you that well. What will happen the first time you and Nick fight?"

My eyes widened as the truth of what I was going to say dawned on me. "What if we never fight?"

Because God had brought us together and we'd invited Him into our relationship, I dared to believe a marriage bound by God *could be* like that. It has been, if "fighting" is defined as raised voices or anger aimed at the other. We certainly do have an occasional disagreement, but I discovered early on in our relationship that I couldn't bear to hurt Nick. I vividly recall the first time I was responsible for a look of hurt that came over his face. I was determined to never be responsible for that look again.

Wives, what we fail to say is just as important as what we do say. Our husbands can't read our minds. From the moment we met, Nick and I were completely transparent and honest with each other, even when that proved uncomfortable or embarrassing, or led to one of those disagreements.

Nick would never have known how important written words were to this wordsmith if I hadn't told him. I could have written him notes and given him cards until I was blue in the face, but until I informed him, in no uncertain terms, that I needed words to make me feel safe, secure, and loved, I'm convinced that all I ever would have gotten from him would be a hand-picked card with the initials NJP, or maybe, if I was lucky, his name spelled out. It would never have been enough.

When it comes to our prayer time however, Nick's prayers for me don't have to be wordy or elaborate. Realizing how vulnerable it is for a man to pray for his wife, a few words from him for me or our marriage suffice. If he lays his hand on me during prayer, it becomes even more powerful. I think any Christian woman would agree there is nothing more attractive than a praying man.

Nick says:

I couldn't believe how important it was to Mary to have my written words. Even with greeting cards, I'd always thought that if the card said what I felt, that was enough. I still take my time choosing the right card for the occasion, one that says what I feel, but now I know to add my own sentiment. The first time I sat down and wrote a letter to Mary, it was difficult to know what to say. I haven't always been good at saying what I mean, and I certainly wasn't used to writing what I felt.

When I saw how much she treasured that first letter I wrote to her as part of her Christmas gift, it made me want to please her that way again, so I always write in her cards and an occasional note, but she's still better at it than me. Sometimes, she'll even write me a card while I'm taking a nap or sitting right next to her watching television!

I've hurt Mary with my words, especially during our first year of marriage. It was never intentional, and I didn't always understand why she was hurt. Either the words had come out wrong, or she was hearing something I didn't really mean. I often excused it, saying I wasn't good with words, but I don't think we can get away with that kind of excuse after we get to know God in a personal way. He can change us.

Mary and I talk about everything, and I mean *everything.* I think we were both surprised at how little we knew about what our first spouses were thinking. Mary would ask, "Well, what did Mindy think about *(whatever)*?" and my truthful answer was, "I don't know." I'd ask what David thought about the same topic, and she'd have the same answer: "I don't know." That isn't right. We should have known. We should have asked and then listened, *really listened* to their answers. I can't go back and change anything, even if I wish I could, but I can make sure not to make the same mistake in my marriage to Mary. She says she feels the same way.

We shared extremely personal things during our first date, so it felt natural to share more as we got to know each other. At some point, Mary started asking, "Tell me a story," every time we were in the car for a length of time. We'd missed out on so much of each other's lives that it was fun to tell background stories about my childhood or teen years. Mary said my baseball and football stories helped her understand my interest in watching sports. Her stories about raising eight children helped me understand her. We still tell each other stories. We also made a pact before we were married that we'd never assume the other would know what we were thinking. Instead, we tell each other.

I'm not sure I've always known how powerful words can be. I've experienced plenty of physical pain in my life, with surgeries and debilitating arthritis. I can handle that, as it's usually temporary, but I've been learning that the pain from verbal digs can cut deep and stay with you.

It's been eye-opening to be on the receiving end of some verbal digs from people I care about and realize I don't want to respond the same way I used to. If I was accused of something, I would feel defensive and argue. Now, I still might feel defensive, but I don't argue. I can say I'm sorry and really mean it.

"Do not let any unwholesome talk come out of your mouths, but only what is helpful for building others up according to their needs, that it may benefit those who listen" (Ephesians 4:29). I think that's pretty good advice when it comes to communication and prayer in marriage too.

DISCUSSION

Gary Chapman, PhD, is a well-known marriage counselor and author of *The 5 Love Languages*.[4] According to Chapman, our "love language" describes how our personality has preferences in giving and receiving love. By learning to recognize those preferences in yourself and each other, you can learn to connect better with your spouse. These five love languages are: words of affirmation, acts of service, receiving gifts, quality time, and physical touch.[5]

1. Take time to do a short questionnaire online to see what your primary love language is. The Love Language® Quiz at: 5lovelanguages.com/quizzes/love-language.

2. Look at the results together. Mary's revealed that hers is physical touch, though she is convinced words of affirmation are just as important to her. Do you agree with your result?

3. Have you been relating to your spouse out of their love language need or yours? Knowing the type of love language your spouse desires, what small action can you take to move in the direction of fulfilling their love language need?

Your words matter. Use these blank pages to take turns writing a short letter to your spouse telling them what personality traits you see in them that makes them special.

His

Hers

Chapter 7

Entertainment Tonight

Finally, brothers and sisters, whatever is true, whatever is noble, whatever is right, whatever is pure, whatever is lovely, whatever is admirable—if anything is excellent or praiseworthy—think about such things.

PHILIPPIANS 4:8

Mary:

While the changes in me in the ten years after my "conversion" might not have looked dramatic on the surface, there was no doubt God was refining me. I began regularly reading the Bible, purposefully praying, and learning to discern God's voice and trust in Him. God was refining me to become the woman Nick Portzen would need in his own transformation after his wife died in 2018.

"Looking for a man who is seeking a personal relationship with God," my dating site profile in the summer of 2021 had been clear, "one willing to pray with me and grow in faith together."

Nick's initial message, affirming that was what he was looking for, resulted in our first meeting. Realizing God had brought us together, we married six weeks later. Growth in our faith was exactly what we experienced as we discovered the difference in a marriage centered on God. We've prayed together daily since that first date, adding a Bible study to our routine in the second year of marriage.

We discovered that the closer we got to God and each other, the greater our transformation, and the more the sins of the world bothered us. We were becoming more like Christ, being conformed to His image, which is exactly what the Bible tells us will happen. "For those God foreknew he also predestined to be conformed to the image of his Son, that he might be the firstborn among many brothers and sisters" (Romans 8:29).

"Be not of this world," we repeatedly read in our Bible studies. We took the admonition seriously, examining our choices in everyday living—what we said, where we went, how we acted, who we hung out with, even down to the forms of entertainment we enjoyed.

Years before I met Nick, I'd already applied moral parameters to my preferred form of entertainment: reading. There were just too many books to choose from to waste time reading anything I considered "garbage." As a librarian, it had been excruciating that I wasn't allowed to screen the books children checked out. It broke my heart when young girls brought a certain set of R-rated books up to the checkout, and I wasn't supposed to say anything. The single time I dared to question the choice of a pre-teen accompanied by her mother, I was horrified by the mother's response. "Of course, I know what she's checking out. I'm going to read them after she is done."

Besides reading books, writing, thrift store shopping, and bike riding, I'd been too busy raising eight children and homeschooling for most of my adult life to pursue other forms of entertainment. Outside of binge-watching television with my youngest daughter every night during the pandemic, I had not watched much television at all.

That changed when I married Nick and discovered how cozy it was to snuggle up on the couch with my new husband and watch television in the evenings. It was with some consternation then that I struggled with a dawning realization that our television viewing was fast becoming a source of discomfort, despite how much we enjoyed that time on the couch together.

If God's goal is that we become more like Christ, then naturally what bothers God should bother us. God abhors sin, and so should we. Abhors is a strong word. God doesn't just dislike sin; it's an abomination to him. The Bible tells us, "To fear the LORD is to hate evil; I hate pride and arrogance, evil behavior and perverse speech" (Proverbs 8:13).

Neither one of us was too keen on the idea that we might need to rethink our television viewing. After all, we were grown-ups, not children. I was reminded of how my mother used to jump up from the couch to cover the television screen with her skirt if she thought something inappropriate was coming up. I'd done much the same with my own young children.

We aren't children. But we are sons and daughters of God. As we matured in our Christian faith, it became increasingly apparent that our lives were to be centered on what pleased God, and there was no denying that some of the shows we watched didn't fit that criterion.

We concluded the only way to decide what pleased our Father was to measure everything according to His Word, meditating on "whatever is noble, whatever is right, whatever is pure, whatever is lovely, whatever is admirable" (Philippians 4:8).

We came up with a plan to make our choices based on the single question: Would we watch this, read that, go there, do this, or have this conversation if Jesus was sitting right next to us? The answer is simple.

Because He is.

As odd as it initially felt consulting parenting websites devoted to rating movies and television shows for families, we found several that helped us make decisions about our television viewing. Dove.org, Movieguide, and the parent guides on the IMDb website proved helpful. Many times, we'd look up a movie that looked good in the trailer, only to discover it included nudity, partial nudity, or frequent swearing and cussing. Though I turned over full control of the remote to Nick, he still asks me to consult reviews of a movie or television shows.

"I don't know. What do you think? Only 159 f-words?" I might report, and we'll laugh about the absurdity of it.

Except it isn't funny. It's a sad commentary on our society that some of the most popular movies and television shows are filled with nudity, obscenities, and immorality. It's even worse that Christians are watching them.

Nick says:

I recently asked Mary why she watched certain shows with me early on in our marriage with no problem, but now there are certain aspects of the same ones she suddenly finds offensive. She thought for a moment before answering, "I think it's because I am seeing things more and more through the eyes of Jesus, and anything sin-related bothers me."

She asked if it used to bother me if a movie had over a hundred f-words in it, and I told her I wouldn't even have noticed. Now? I notice if there is one. Then she asked if something happened to her, would I go back to my old television-viewing habits? I had to think about that. Honestly, there have been times I worried I might not have anything left to watch if we continued to screen our entertainment! But then I realized that my tastes have changed. Even without Mary, I would still be a discerning viewer out of respect for her and God.

Entertainment was never just about television for me. I grew up interested in sports—watching it on television but also playing. I played basketball, baseball, softball, and football through elementary and high school and continued playing softball as an adult, until I blew out a knee. Then it was bowling and golf for years. For a while, I was in bowling leagues four nights a week, with double shifts on Wednesday nights. I took great pride in my bowling skills and had the awards to prove it. By the time I met Mary, I'd given up bowling because of nerve damage and arthritis that extended from my hand to the length of my arm and shoulder, so she never knew me as an award-winning bowler.

Still, I liked to relive my glory days, visiting with league players at my place of business, where Mary would get a glimpse of what some of those leagues were like. There were times when we visited the bowling center on league night, and I'd suggest she stay in the office while I visited with old friends. On the way home, Mary would ask why I wanted her to stay in the office. I told her the truth; I said I knew the coarse language and crude jokes would bother her. I was used to it, so it didn't really bother me at first, even after I'd stopped contributing to it.

Neither one of us remembers exactly what Mary said that hurt me once, but I have an idea. I owned an expensive and pretty impressive gold ring for bowling a 300 game. Mary and I had been married almost two years when I was on speaker phone with my sister, and she mentioned how her husband had made a piece of jewelry for her from one of his rings. I thought I saw Mary's eyes light up at that comment, so I quickly said, "Don't get any ideas. I wouldn't get rid of my 300 ring for anyone, not even you."

Her eyes definitely reacted to that comment. Noting the deep hurt I caused, I quickly got off the phone, determined to explain just how much the ring meant to me, how hard I'd worked for it, and how prestigious it was to bowl a 300 game.

"If you loved me, you wouldn't even ask me to get rid of such a ring," I told her, but nothing I said calmed her down.

"I wasn't asking you to give up a ring. I don't even want jewelry made from your ring," she insisted. What she couldn't believe was that I would put a piece of jewelry above a person. She went on and on for what felt like half the afternoon, questioning my attachment to a piece of jewelry, wondering how I could put something material above a person I professed to love.

I didn't like her line of reasoning—certain I was in the right about this but becoming less certain as she continued. There was no yelling or raised voices in our disagreement; there was just a lot of hurt and misunderstanding. If I remember correctly, it was a comment from her questioning my faith that really hurt me.

What did faith have to do with a ring, I wondered. But the more I thought about it, the more I realized how my pride did get in the way of my relationship with Mary *and* God. A few days later, I ended up selling that ring, proving to myself, God, and Mary that no material item had that kind of hold on me.

A similar conversation ensued after I sold the business and carted home stacks of award plaques. What would we do with all of them? For a while, a bulletin board full of bowling tournament patches hung on a door in our home office. The plaques stayed in boxes in the garage until we packed for a move, when Mary came up with the idea of keeping a few and taking photos of the others. She organized the bowling tournament patches and photos of the plaques in a black leather binder she labeled "Nick's bowling."

Done. And done. Except the topic of pride came up again when Mary was unpacking. Her daughter had made letters with the covers of her books spelling out the word "WRITER" along with a cross symbol with her latest book cover on it.

"What's the difference between hanging up my bowling awards and you hanging up the word WRITER with your book covers on?" I asked her. "Isn't that prideful too?"

I regretted my words as soon as I said them because, unlike me with my defensive attitude about the bowling ring, Mary took my words to heart, spending several days agonizing over the decision of whether to hang up the letters. She reminded me she'd taken down a book award the day we'd talked about my ring for fear of seeming prideful.

Mary prayed and journaled for several days before concluding that her books point people to God, so displaying the covers in the unique way her daughter had come up with would serve as a conversation starter to talk about faith and God.

Could my bowling awards do the same? Had I ever thanked God or attributed my bowling prowess to God? Mary had asked me some form of that question many times as she was exposed to more and more of the potential negative aspects of belonging to a league.

"Are there religious organizations that form teams?" she'd ask, or "Do all leagues include drinking and coarse joking?"

After a visit to a unique aquarium-themed bowling center in Altoona, Iowa, Mary wondered why my inquiry of, "Do you have bowling leagues here?" was answered by an employee with, "No, of course not; we're a family business."

Gulp. That didn't help matters. I'd always considered *my* business a family one, taken great pride in that fact. *There's that word again. Pride.*

I thought about how my dad had bowled as a form of entertainment, belonging to a Catholic men's league. How my brother Pat had gone bowling with church members. Bowling itself wasn't sinful.

It wasn't until the summer of 2024, as we were working on this book, that this question came up. *Would I have invited Jesus to join my bowling league?*

I met a lot of Christian men in our new community, men who had been following Jesus a lot longer than me. One of them professed to accept Jesus as his Savior at the age of eight. Impressed by my bowling skills, he brought up the topic of my perfect 300 games among a group of other Christian men. One asked how it felt when I had nine strikes in a row and went into the tenth frame. He mentioned his best game was when the doctor had prescribed codeine for a cold, and he'd relaxed enough to bowl a near-perfect game.

Suddenly, I was ashamed. I'd been drinking all night when I'd scored the perfect game. I'd been drunk, sobering up fast, facing that last frame. I always drank a lot back then, probably more than anyone knew. Could I admit that to these perfect Christian men?

I'd never thought much about my drinking. It was just another form of entertainment for me. I drank hard, but I worked hard. I provided for my family, never got mean or violent. I even used to joke, "I'm not an alcoholic. I know because I've never gone to an AA meeting." Ha. Ha.

I told those good Christian men I didn't want to talk about my bowling awards—because I was ashamed. "I wasn't a very good man back then," I confessed. "I drank. A lot. I wasn't a Christian then."

This group of faith-filled men didn't judge me. Instead, they gathered around me and spoke only loving, non-judgmental words. One admitted to some problem behavior as a youth. Another said he'd turned away from God for a while during an unwanted divorce. One told me my past didn't matter; I'd been forgiven. It was my present and future that mattered.

Would I have invited Jesus to join my bowling league? Maybe one of them, but definitely not the others. My advice now to any man, young or old, before you join any group, whether it's a baseball team, a bowling league, or a men's group, is to find out what the members are like. What kind of things do they do together? What are their morals and values? Will they bring you closer to God or pull you away? This is important because we become like the people we spend the most time with.

And if you someday find yourself in a group or on a team and realize it isn't making you a better person, get out. It isn't worth your soul to stay in.

DISCUSSION

Do not conform to the pattern of this world but be transformed by the renewing of your mind. Then you will be able to test and approve what God's will is— his good, pleasing and perfect will.

Romans 12:2

"Sorry, Mary. I'm still going to watch my favorite R-rated show. It's my one guilty pleasure," a friend commented when I mentioned our decision to look at all entertainment through God's eyes. I don't know why she was apologizing to me. Instead, she might consider the ramifications of what she'd just said. *Guilty pleasure.*

1. Do you have a "guilty pleasure" in your life? Maybe it is in the food you eat, your drinking, your reading material, the movies or television shows you watch, places you go, or events you attend. Ask yourself if the pleasure makes it worth the guilt.

2. Would you be willing to invite Jesus to join you in your television-watching or favorite activities?

3. How are you different from "the world?" Would someone who doesn't know you very well be able to tell you are a Christian from the way you act or talk, or do you act and sound like everyone else?

Pray together:

Lord Jesus Christ, we want to be more like You. Please guide us in our lives so we may honor You in all our choices in entertainment and activities. Let us glorify You in all that we do. Let others see You in us. Let our lives reflect You.

Chapter 8

Holy Sex

I found the one my heart loves. I held him and would not let him go.

Song of Solomon 3:4

Mary:

Looking back, Nick and I marvel at the deep connection we felt, how we'd shared intimate details of our life in the two hours of our first meeting, before we'd even hugged. Certainly, before we'd held hands or shared a kiss. Why? What possible explanation was there for that kind of transparency between two virtual strangers?

It had to be from God. While our culture has romanticized the notion of "soul mates" and the idea that there is one perfect person out there, how often is the *soul* considered in the relationship? From a biblical standpoint, a true "soul mate" means a relationship that includes God.

In the years before I'd met Nick, I prayed that God would protect my heart. He'd honored that request, making it clear when someone wasn't part of His plan for me, so I trusted He would quickly reveal whether Nick was. Our correspondence before our first meeting consisted of texts, emails, and a single phone call. It was clear Nick was actively seeking something that was missing in his life, the personal relationship with God I'd developed. If there had been any indication Nick wasn't open to growing in faith, I never would have agreed to meet him because I was so close to God by then. I remember the moment I spotted Nick walking up the steps to my house, the distinct feeling of already knowing him, as if our souls recognized each other, which could explain our comfort level with each other.

By praying together before our second date, Nick and I added to that the spiritual component of our relationship. We were pleasantly surprised then to discover God had gifted us with an incredible chemistry as well, something we'd never expected at our age. Our desire for physical affection matched that of our emotional connection. A waitress at the local diner we frequented for breakfast confided that the employees there had dubbed us "the lovebirds" because we held hands while we drank coffee as we waited for our meal to be served. Before we got married, we'd needed to consult a chiropractor for neck pain because of the odd angle that kissing in a vehicle necessitated.

It was natural, then, that we would broach the topic of marital intimacy from a Christian perspective. Even though I assumed God would delight in and bless our union, I still had concerns.

Having been with only one man my entire adult life, it was a bit disconcerting as a sixty-one-year-old widow to imagine beginning a new sexual relationship. After all, my first husband had aged with me, our bodies changing in sync. My three C-sections, a gall bladder removal, and hernia surgery had left my abdomen scarred. I no longer had the body of a twenty-year-old.

Then again, neither did sixty-eight-year-old Nick, who assured me it didn't matter, that he found me beautiful. His own abdomen sported scars from previous surgeries. Still, as our wedding day approached, I worried my husband would be disappointed and disillusioned.

I turned to the Bible, searching for what it had to say about the husband and wife cleaving unto one another and "becoming one flesh." What did God's Word have to say about sex?

Plenty, it turned out. To prepare for our wedding night, I read the Song of Solomon out loud in the car one day. Midway through, Nick turned to me with widened eyes, his face a bit flushed.

"Is that saying what I think it is saying?" he asked. I assured him it was. The couple featured in these passages were enjoying each other in unbridled passion.

The Bible says, "Take delight in the LORD, and he will give you the desires of your heart." (Psalm 37:4). God designed sex. He delights in a husband and wife finding joy in each other. Unfortunately, neither Nick nor I had even considered God in our previous marital beds. Instead, sex seemed something separate from anything spiritual.

When Nick and I made the mutual decision to invite God into our bedroom on our wedding night, we had no idea just what that could mean for our relationship, but God greatly blessed our physical union.

Thanking God for each other while in bed has become the standard for our satisfying sex life, and that's just how God wants it. That we never invited Him into that aspect of our previous marriages is one of our biggest regrets. The fact is that it never once occurred to us that the designer of sex might want to be a part of the gift He's given married couples. Not as a voyeur but as conductor, the maestro of the majesty of the symphony of the sexual union.

One caveat: Wives, I need to make a confession and give a gentle warning. I was alone for a long time before I met Nick, nine and a half years, to be exact. During that time, I met many widows and widowers who'd found love again, and I envied them. There were times I wondered if there was something wrong with me because I hadn't, thinking I might be unlovable. Those thoughts and feelings were not from God but the Evil One.

In those darkest days, I turned to God. There were many lonely nights when I lay in bed, clutching a wooden comfort cross, praying through my tears, asking God to bring me the man He'd promised me, or take the desire to be loved away.

When I met Nick, I fell head over heels in love. I had no doubt he was a gift from above. I thanked God every day for this magnificent man He'd brought into my life. I still do. I was totally enamored with Nick. That didn't dissipate after we were married. On the contrary, my love grew stronger with each passing day. I was three years into our marriage before I realized I was looking less to God and more to Nick to fill the deep corners of my heart. My husband and our physical intimacy were fast becoming idols in my life.

Our God wants us to put Him first, above all things, even those good things He blesses us with. He wants no idols before Him. God used the six-week recovery period after my cancer surgery and several episodes of back pain when physical intimacy wasn't possible to remind me I was to rely on Him, not Nick, to meet my needs. Nick is, indeed, a gift from God, as is our incredible chemistry, but neither was ever meant to be put above God.

Nick says:

Ditto. What she said. Except the part about me being a god to Mary. As much as I love her, I've never put my relationship with Mary above God.

I was a little embarrassed at first when I found out that the waitresses at a café called us "the lovebirds" because we held hands while drinking coffee. Mary is very affectionate. I liked that she wanted to hold my hand all the time, but I definitely wasn't used to it.

I'll never forget the first time Mary kissed me in public. I was holding the car door open for her when she took my face in her hands and gave me a big kiss. I remember looking around to see who might have seen us, not because I was ashamed. Maybe a little embarrassed, but more because I wasn't accustomed to public displays of affection.

It took me a few months to realize what I'd never actually admitted to myself: I'd always craved more physical affection. It was no surprise then when the Love Languages® quiz mentioned in a previous chapter revealed my love language to be physical touch. God gave me that tenfold when he brought me Mary.

When a nurse at the VA clinic asked us if we were newlyweds, it made me realize that people weren't used to seeing older couples holding hands or treating each other the way we do. Mary has always said she wants to have the kind of marriage where people will be asking us in fifteen years if we are newlyweds. I think we'll shoot for that goal.

DISCUSSION

Love is patient, love is kind. It does not envy, it does not boast, it is not proud. It does not dishonor others, it is not self-seeking, it is not easily angered, it keeps no record of wrongs. Love does not delight in evil but rejoices with the truth. It always protects, always trusts, always hopes, always perseveres.

1 Corinthians 13:4–7

1. Does your marriage reflect the kind of love described in this Bible verse? If not, what might you need to work on as a couple?

2. Do you treasure your spouse? How does (or doesn't) your attitude reflect that they are one of your greatest gifts?

3. Make a list on the following blank pages of gestures, words, gifts or actions that make you feel special.

4. Look at each other's lists. Any surprises? Is there something you can do this week from that list to show your spouse how much you love them?

His

Hers

Chapter 9

Awe-Inspired

The whole earth is filled with awe at your wonders; where morning dawns, where evening fades, you call forth songs of joy.

Psalm 65:8

Mary:

I was raised in poverty and didn't escape it for most of my adult life. Growing up as the seventh of ten children and then raising my own eight children on mostly one income, there simply wasn't a lot of money, no matter how hard my dad or David worked. Yet, I'd never felt as though I lacked for anything important. My goal as a mother had never been to give my children things I never had but, instead, to give them what I *did* have, a mother's loving presence, a sense of stability, and faith.

Call me naïve, but it never once occurred to me that my children were missing something without college funds, family vacations, or experiences others might take for granted. I didn't feel as if I or my children missed out on anything that really counted, at least not regarding getting to heaven. Nor did I experience envy of others for their vehicles, homes, vacations, or ability to purchase things that were out of my financial reach. The only way envy crept into my life was my perception of the free time other women seemed to have. I envied those who did not have to struggle to make ends meet or feel a sense of urgency to contribute to their family's income.

I'd always thought I'd done a good job of hiding any discontent from my children, never wanting them or their father to know how desperate I sometimes felt about a need to contribute something, *anything*, to our income. That desperation meant getting up at 5:00 a.m. to write articles I could sell for twenty-five dollars or spending weeks, even months, collecting enough coupons and free tokens so my children could enjoy an afternoon of fun at Chuck E. Cheese, what we dubbed "Family Fun Day." Even then, it seemed I couldn't just relax and enjoy the day. No, I'd bring my well-stocked coupon box for a huge coupon spree afterward or stop at a thrift store where I'd pick up clothing and books to sell online. Our day trips always included Mom's couponing or thrift-shopping prowess so I could make or save money.

Only recently did one of my daughters mention how "frantic" I'd always seemed as a mother. My heart sank at her comment. For all the positive I'd hoped to impart to my children, they'd still glimpsed a negative aspect of poverty. The fact was, until I was widowed and inherited a modest life insurance policy and social security for my remaining children, we'd always qualified for some form of government program, whether it was WIC or heat assistance. It wasn't until 2012, at the age of fifty-two, with four children remaining at home, that I was thrust to a level of income where I didn't qualify for any government assistance. I felt positively rich.

For eighteen months after David's death, I was able to relax a little, experiencing the solitude and silence that grieving required. I abandoned two very part-time jobs and spent much of that first year writing or doing only those workshops that would allow me to include my youngest daughter. She and I traveled to libraries all over Iowa to do couponing workshops.

Within that slower-paced interim, I learned to savor each moment, paying more attention to the world around me, the beautiful, wonderful, painful, and broken world I lived in as I grieved a mother and husband and watched my grandson Jacob fight a losing battle with cancer.

That little boy taught me so much about the fragility of life. He lived, *really lived*, each and every day, bravely facing treatment that would bring grown men to their knees. I never felt closer to God than I did during the months when Jacob was dying. Every sense heightened, I'd find myself gazing out the window as I did dishes, pausing to watch birds gathering at the feeder. I fully experienced the cooling effect of a soft breeze on the back of my neck as I rode my bicycle in the summer heat. The pungent scent of fresh-mown grass brought me to tears. I'd lift my face toward the warmth of the sunshine, soaking it in. I'd gasp at the beauty of a rainbow, the colors more vivid than any I'd ever seen. I'd watch the sun set on the horizon then get up early to see it rise.

That sense of awe I experienced over simple things never waned, even after the life insurance money was gone and I needed to seek work. I felt God's guidance in each job he brought me to, from the first as a library director, where I was allowed to bring my young daughters with me, to a position a few years later at a spirituality center where I could freely share my faith. Every morning, I woke up excited, wondering how God might use me that day.

By the time I met Nick, I'd had seven books published, developed a public speaking ministry, obtained a grief counseling certificate, headed annual grief and writing conferences, and was earning more than twenty-five dollars an hour at my day job. I was well aware that only God could have brought me to that point, and none of it was because of me.

It was important to me that Nick know I wasn't dating him because he was a successful businessman. On the contrary, his apparent success initially made me nervous, even though, by all accounts, I could also be deemed "successful." The difference in our expectations and experience when it came to finances came to a head very soon after we met when Nick took me to a supper club to meet his children. He made it clear it was his treat, a gesture that sent me searching for the cheapest item on the menu while everyone else seemed to have no qualms ordering whatever they wanted, including expensive drinks. Nauseated at the staggering amount, I had to look away when Nick signed the credit card statement that included a hefty tip. I knew, without a doubt, what my children would have done in the same situation. Knowing he was paying, they would have searched for the least expensive item, even if that meant macaroni and cheese from the kids' menu.

I didn't immediately reveal my shock. At home that night, I unpacked my strong emotions through prayer and journaling, even calling my oldest daughter to help me sort through my feelings. I had a difficult time sleeping that night. *Could a man who casually dropped that amount of money on a meal for his family truly understand a woman who spent twenty dollars or less for two people on the rare times she went out? A woman, who up until 2012, never spent more than $1500 on a vehicle, and then only when a tax refund was available? Could he appreciate a mother who'd dumpster-dived and traipsed through alleys collecting proofs of purchase to provide Christmas gifts of company premiums such as stuffed animals, balls, and T-shirts for her eight children with her couponing and refunding hobby? Had Nick ever purchased secondhand furniture or clothing, or was he used to buying everything new?* Bottom line: *Could he even appreciate simple things?*

The next morning, Nick listened patiently to my litany of concerns, addressing them as a man who took pride in his ability to not only take care of his family but also provide material items he hadn't had when he was younger.

When it came to life experiences, our differences were even more pronounced. Nick was widely traveled, having been all over the United States for business, bowling tournaments, and vacations with his family or alone with his wife. I, on the other hand, had never taken a vacation, never traveled for fun except twice in the years before I met him. I'd flown to Florida to visit my sister and brother-in-law in 2017, and my children gave me gifts of cash the following Christmas so I could fly in 2019 to visit my daughter and son-in-law and meet my new grandson in California. Those trips exposed me to things I'd never seen before, ocean beaches and a mountain, reminding me of this verse: "For since the creation of the world God's invisible qualities—his eternal power and divine nature—have been clearly seen, being understood from what has been made, so that people are without excuse" (Romans 1:20). How anyone could see such a beautiful masterpiece and not recognize God in it was beyond me.

If Nick did take things for granted when we met, he would soon be confronted with a dose of reality. One Sunday before we were married, my brother-in-law called to invite us for a Sunday afternoon drive. Seated in their back seat, my head on Nick's shoulder, his hand clutched in mine, I pondered how different our lives had been, how different mine had been from my older sister's too. Joan remembered Sunday afternoon drives with Mom and Dad. By the time I was born, there was too little time, too little money, and too many children for the luxury of those drives. It had been the same for me and David. Even if we'd had the gas money, our youngest children were terrible travelers. A Sunday afternoon car ride would have been torture, not pleasure. No, I'd never experienced the joy of a Sunday afternoon drive.

By the time Joan and Dave dropped us off, I was choking back sobs. It took me a while to explain to Nick that the crying was good, in appreciation for the opportunity to experience something other people took for granted. That appreciation would morph into pure awe after we were married and Nick and I took our first cross-country trip through several states, including stops in Colorado and New Mexico, before landing in Arizona, where his sister lived.

My seasoned traveler husband—used to road trips and beautiful scenery—would glance over at me, see tears streaming down my face, and naturally wonder what was wrong.

"Are you okay?" he'd ask before eventually learning to tell the difference between "good" tears and bad. I cried all the time on trips, choking up at the beauty of God's creation. I still do. Nick calls me a "crybaby," but his eyes soften, and he smiles when he does.

Everything was new to me: restaurant chains I'd never heard about, the variety of gift shops and tourist attractions, places and things Nick was accustomed to. I was especially fascinated by the machines that smashed pennies into shiny, flat pieces of memorabilia that I started collecting everywhere we went. I bought a United States bulletin board, marking the states we traveled with colored pins.

I wake up in awe of each day, even the ordinary ones. Especially the ordinary ones. I glance over at Nick, grateful for yet another day with him. My attitude must be pleasing to our Lord, considering the words of Jesus: "And he said: 'Truly

I tell you, unless you change and become like little children, you will never enter the kingdom of heaven'" (Matthew 18:3). I'm behaving exactly how God wants me to, caught up in childlike wonder of our beautiful world, enjoying the simplest things, and appreciating every moment with my husband. I cry every day.

The "good" kind of crying.

Nick says:

Mary was right. By the time I met her, I did take material things for granted. I didn't consider myself wealthy, but if I wanted something, I just bought it. As an example, I remember working on a project of some sort in the garage or at my business, knowing I already owned the tools I needed. But when I couldn't find them right away, I'd go buy more.

If I wanted leather gloves or a nice leather coat, I'd go to a store, usually an expensive one, and buy whatever I wanted. I didn't even compare prices. I assumed quality cost more and was worth it. I figured I worked hard and deserved whatever I purchased.

I don't want to say I felt sorry for Mary and her lack of experience, because that sounds like I didn't appreciate how it made her more sensitive to things, but I did feel bad for her when she told me she hadn't experienced something as simple as a Sunday afternoon drive. I'd just assumed everyone would have done that. Mary's sensitivity is one of the qualities that attracted me to her in the first place, but when she started crying over the simplest things, it bothered me at first. That is, until I realized her tears were from happiness and appreciation. Now, if Mary doesn't cry at least once a day, I feel as though I've failed her in some way.

I'm not making fun of her, because we laugh together about this now, but on our first big road trip, we stopped at a Cracker Barrel restaurant six or seven hours from home. I was surprised at her reaction to the gift shop. To me, it was like any other gift shop with overpriced clothes and gift items. She told me to call her phone when our meal was delivered, and then she headed straight to the clearance shelves while I relaxed and drank coffee. She was smiling when she joined me at the table, excited about the items she'd found for Christmas gifts for me and her children. The only thing that dimmed her joy was the fact that she'd just spent half the money she'd brought for souvenirs on the first day of our trip! I'd never thought to advise Mary on how much money she should bring for a ten-day trip, with stops in Colorado Springs, Sante Fe, New Mexico, and several days in Arizona. Apparently, she considered $200 a large amount of money to bring but then spent half of that in the first gift shop she visited. I shouldn't have laughed, but I did, and so did she. I'm glad she can laugh at herself! But I also felt sorry for her not having vacation experience so that she would realize how much souvenirs could cost. I noticed she started collecting touristy smashed pennies, fridge magnets, and mugs after that valuable lesson.

Mary was like a little kid in the candy store, a kid who'd never had candy, and suddenly, they get a piece and they're crying because it tastes so good. That is Mary. I loved watching her delight at the littlest things. After we went on our second big trip that first year of marriage, Mary asked me what else was on my bucket list. I told her the truth; the only thing on my bucket list was to see more places through her eyes.

Mary's outlook made me look at material items differently too. I'll never forget the time she walked into a consignment store, determined to show me she could find a leather coat for herself without spending much. I don't know what I expected her to come out with, but it wasn't a brand-new women's leather jacket with tags still attached that she paid twenty-five dollars for! I still haven't gotten to where I enjoy the thrift-shopping experience myself, but I'm impressed by some of the things Mary finds.

My concept of money and how much I needed to retire on changed when we started praying specifically for God to guide us in the sale of my business. Mary affectionately called me Scrooge McDuck sometimes, having seen me crunching numbers with a calculator and stacks of bills at my desk. All I needed was a visor and a cigar, she'd joke.

Once I was semi-retired, it became clear that my idea to retire with piles of money and spend my days golfing didn't mesh with reality. With interest rates sky-high I wasn't going to be getting a pile of money for my business anytime soon, and with my bad arthritis, it didn't look good for my golf game either. Mary kept reminding me that God knew exactly what we needed for retirement and had plans way beyond golf for me.

Now that the business is sold and I'm on more of a fixed income with social security, my ideas about spending money have changed too. I can't just buy whatever I want anymore, and I wouldn't anyway. I've learned to seek God's guidance in how we spend money. I still like to go out for a good meal occasionally, but I think twice before spending so much.

Now, I can appreciate the littlest things. I love how Mary wakes up cheerful every morning. She delivers my first cup of coffee with a kiss, what she calls a "coffee kiss," so my first taste of coffee is from her lips after she takes a drink from her cup. We spend the first hour of every morning doing a Bible study or reading from a devotional. We might take a walk or enjoy an hour of water walking at a local pool. In the afternoons, I find myself gazing out the window, watching birds at our feeders, something I never imagined doing. This must be what it means to be a joyful Christian, with a joy that can only come from within.

DISCUSSION

"Blessed are the poor in spirit, for theirs is the kingdom of heaven."
MATTHEW 5:3

1. Mary's lack of money meant she may have missed out on some of the finer "material" items for most of her life, but she is convinced she lacked for nothing important. (Except maybe time). Poverty, in monetary terms, is one thing, but what do you think it means to be "poor in spirit?"

2. Nick discovered his ideas about spending money changed when he learned to seek God's guidance in his spending. What is your opinion on stewardship? Have you allowed God to guide you in your spending?

Pray this prayer together:

Lord, thank you for the blessings You have bestowed upon us. We want to be good stewards of our money. We ask for Your Holy Spirit to give us discernment regarding how we spend, save, and share our money with others. Let us never become so jaded that we don't appreciate the little things.

Chapter 10

Fruit of the Spirit

"And I will ask the Father, and he will give you another advocate to be with you forever—the Spirit of truth. The world cannot accept him, because it neither sees him nor knows him. But you know him, for he lives with you and will be in you. I will not leave you as orphans; I will come to you."

JOHN 14:16–18

In the same way, the Spirit helps us in our weakness. We do not know what we ought to pray for, but the Spirit himself intercedes for us through wordless groans. And he who searches our hearts knows the mind of the Spirit, because the Spirit intercedes for God's people in accordance with the will of God.

ROMANS 8:26–27

Mary:

We open this chapter with two Bible verses regarding the Holy Spirit because this topic is so important. Understanding the gift we are given when we begin following Jesus is crucial to our walk with Christ. I know I didn't always understand what it meant to have the Spirit within me.

Depending on the version of the Bible, the Holy Spirit is described as counselor, comforter, advocate, or helper. When we invite Jesus into our lives, he sends us His Holy Spirit, who guides, instructs, and encourages us in our faith.

I sensed the presence of the Spirit before I had an explanation for it. A year after David died, I stood before a church congregation to announce I was beginning a Bible study. I can't remember much of my twenty-minute talk, but I know I spoke of how losing both a mother and a husband and facing the impending loss of a grandson had led me to God's Word and the comfort I'd found in studying the Bible. What I do remember is looking up from my notes and seeing people wiping away tears. I'd done a little public speaking by then, hosting extreme couponing workshops for libraries and community colleges, but this was the first time I realized the power of words to reach the hearts of others, and I knew, without a doubt, that power source had not come from me but through me.

From that point on, I prayed for God to use me however He wanted in my capacity as a Bible study leader, speaker, or presenter. He was orchestrating my life in ways I would never have imagined.

In the ensuing years, I'd speak to support groups and churches about finding hope in grief. I flew to Dallas, Texas, to speak to grieving parents at a Compassionate Friends conference—simply because my daughter asked me to. There, I met a man who spoke on signs from beyond. He agreed to travel to Iowa to speak at a grief retreat I'd felt led to organize. I didn't immediately attribute these kinds of divine summons to the Holy Spirit working in me, even though I had no idea what I'd say to grieving parents and was not even remotely qualified to lead Bible studies or organize retreats. I just obeyed the directive.

It's one thing to have followed God for twelve years—through multiple deaths, raising three girls as a single mom, job hunts, and years of loneliness. To have developed a personal relationship with a God who became my Father in every imaginable way, experiencing His presence through the good, the bad, and even the ugly (because I admit, there was a lot of ugly crying associated with the transformation). It's another to understand the gift God gave me in the form of a Spirit who has guided me every step of the way.

I'd known good faith-filled people but didn't recognize what I know now was the Holy Spirit within them. My mother was one of them, her life demonstrating the fruit of the Spirit mentioned in Galatians 5:22–25: love, joy, peace, forbearance, kindness, goodness, faithfulness, gentleness, and self-control.

The Bible explains my lack of understanding this way: "The person without the Spirit does not accept the things that come from the Spirit of God but considers them foolishness, and cannot understand them because they are discerned only through the Spirit" (1 Corinthians 2:14).

When did I begin to understand the Spirit dwelling within me? I'm not sure I realized it was the Holy Spirit urging me to pray for my future husband in 2018. It was years after I developed a personal relationship with God that I recognized the Spirit working in Nick. Only then did I recognize how the Spirit had guided me in a similar way into public speaking ministry and in establishing grief events I wasn't at all qualified to organize and implement. How He'd guided my writing. Ah, yes, the writing. It is not lofty to credit this book to the One who guided it to fruition.

I've learned to depend on the Holy Spirit to guide, encourage, instruct, and convict me of sin that remains in me. Back in 2015, struggling with a delight in gossip, I'd asked my Bible study group to pray I'd have the strength to defeat that vice. By the time I met Nick, I thought I had my tendency to gossip under control, only to have it rear its ugly head again after I married him. It seemed his work environment was rife with gossip. I could easily avoid most of it, but soon, realized I took way too much enjoyment in the bad-mouthing of someone who had treated Nick badly. Once, I even caught myself adding to it and immediately felt sick.

That nausea? It's an all-too-familiar gut reaction to sin now as I become more like Jesus and less like gossipy me. I appreciate the physical discomfort because I know it is the Holy Spirit reminding me of everything I've learned as a Christ follower. I know now to respond by nipping any negative talk before it goes too far.

I've wrestled with the Spirit on occasion when I don't understand something I'm prompted to do. I wrestled with Him on that June day in 2018 when I was instructed to pray for my future husband, because I didn't dare believe there would *be* a future husband. I wrestled with the Spirit when I was led to leave a good-paying job, a move that didn't make sense to me at the time. When I prayed for a clear sign of guidance, He gave me three instead. In the space of one week, three different people came to my office with words that made my decision clear. What followed, with my husband needing me at his workplace, convinced me to always trust in the guidance of the Holy Spirit.

When I don't immediately obey those divine prompts, I regret it. Once, it was a homeless man eating cold hot dogs straight from the package outside a convenience store. Our eyes met briefly as I left the store, and I saw Jesus in his. I was so overwhelmed by the sight that I retreated to my car and sobbed. By the time I composed myself to offer him the cash in my purse, he was gone. I don't let those opportunities pass me by anymore, and I'm married to a man who is the same. We try not to question prompts from the Holy Spirit, even if they don't always make sense at the time.

When we do fail to obey, we give each other grace, reminding ourselves and each other we are works in progress, continuing to mature and grow in faith. Ultimately, my goal is to have others see Him in my actions, hear Him in my words. "More of Him, less of me" has become my mantra.

I must be doing something right. It wasn't long ago I was making small talk with a woman as we stood in line at a book signing. We'd been discussing loved ones who we were worried about.

She suddenly exclaimed, "Your smile!"

What about my smile? I wondered. *Do I have something between my teeth?*

I must have looked alarmed because she hurried to add, "When you smiled, I saw Jesus in you."

I burst into tears. She reached out to hug me.

Two strangers, in public, holding each other as we both cried. Now, that's the Holy Spirit.

Nick says:

I'd heard of the Holy Spirit but never really understood who He was or how He worked. When I met Mary, I was already searching for something I knew was missing in my life. I didn't know what that was until she talked about having a personal relationship with God. I'd heard people use the term "born-again Christian" before but didn't really know what that meant either; I may even have made fun of someone using that phrase.

Listening to Mary, I realized she'd made a conscious choice to follow Jesus. She didn't just talk about faith. She was living what she talked about. When I made the choice to get to know God in a personal way, it was kind of like when I quit a forty-year habit of chewing tobacco. It had to be me making the choice and sticking with it for it to work, to really "take." I wasn't going to change for someone else. I had to change for myself.

When I first started reading the Bible, I didn't understand a lot of it, but the more I studied Scripture, the more I got out of it. When I learned the Holy Spirit dwells in us when we begin following Jesus and we can depend on him to guide us, it made perfect sense how easy it had been to stop cussing or abandon other bad habits.

When Mary and I got married, she'd say things like, "You're going to write a book with me someday," or she'd predict we'd do speeches together. I couldn't understand how she could be so sure that would happen. I had gotten such bad grades in high school and am a terrible speller. I certainly didn't see myself as a public speaker!

Then I remembered how I'd spoken in front of groups as a former Tavern League county president and Tavern League state director who traveled nine counties to speak to groups. It had been easy to talk to those groups because I had an interest in the rules and regulations as a bar owner. I really knew my stuff, even memorizing many of the bylaws. I took pride (*there's that word again*) that people called me for answers to their questions.

If I could memorize and talk about tavern bylaws and regulations, why would I doubt my ability to learn Bible verses and talk about faith? When I discovered our speaking styles were similar in that both Mary and I preferred to speak from an outline or notes, I became more confident we could comfortably speak together, and I was right.

Think about the unlikelihood of that for a minute: a former Tavern League director speaking on faith! If the Holy Spirit could guide me to do that, then why not an ability to write on the same topic? Mary knew what I was capable of long before I did, insisting God equips those He calls.

And He did. When we first started working on this book together, we thought my part would be maybe a single paragraph following hers. Then one day, when Mary read one of my paragraphs out loud to me, I realized I had more to add. I started talking, and Mary began writing as fast as she could, jotting down everything I was saying. Before we knew it, we'd added two pages to that one paragraph. That happened with nearly every chapter!

There's a lot that has changed in my life these past few years because I have been equipped with the power of the Holy Spirit, things I would never have imagined. I never thought I'd become a discerning television watcher or curb my language. I never imagined becoming the kind of man who would enjoy simple things like sitting and watching birds and squirrels in the backyard or playing cards with my wife.

Once I made the choice to follow God, it had to be the Holy Spirit who led me to move away from the environment where I'd made a living for more than thirty years. What I hadn't expected was that He would lead me even farther away from that community. One hour away, I'd still run into old buddies who'd known me in my party days, constant reminders of who I'd been. Still, I never imagined moving again. Yet God had other ideas.

In June 2023, Mary and I rented a beautiful cabin on the grounds of Riverview Ministries in Cedar Falls while we ran the Christian Writers conference there. For the three days we stayed, we'd wake up every morning marveling at how beautiful the house was. We both said the same thing, "If this ever came up for sale, we'd buy it in a heartbeat." We meant it too. The atmosphere was relaxing, warm, and comfortable, with wooden beams and pine wainscoting.

It was a pipe dream. We never expected it to come true. Yet something in us (the Holy Spirit?) led us to fill out paperwork and submit our faith statements to the Riverview office that December. In January, Mary visited the cabin owner's Facebook Page to ask if her cabin would be available again in June. They'd become Facebook friends after our stay, briefly sharing some of their mutual faith stories. The owner was a widow, and her husband had designed the cabin. Mary was horrified to see the woman's obituary posted on her Facebook Page. We didn't discuss the implications, but Mary admitted to a familiar feeling, a sense that something was happening.

Three months later, we got the call. The cabin was up for sale. Were we interested? We definitely were. We knelt to pray right after that phone call. We'd been praying every day of our marriage, but that's the first time we knelt to do so! I have a hard time getting up off the floor once I'm down. From that prayer on, it had to be the Holy Spirit guiding our way because we felt as though God was orchestrating everything, even down to a dream we both had one night. When Mary woke up one morning and said she'd dreamed we were living in the cabin, I was astounded. I'd dreamed the same thing!

"Well, in my dream, you were driving a golf cart around the neighborhood, doing daily rounds," she continued with a laugh. We couldn't believe it. I'd been doing the same thing in my dream!

The house showing had to be the oddest one in the history of house showings because we spent more time talking about faith than we did peeking in closets. We just knew the house was for us. In fact, on the way home, after our offer was accepted, Mary called her friend Mary to tell her we bought it.

"What color is the siding?" her friend asked, and Mary looked at me. I shrugged. "I don't know." She answered with a laugh.

She laughed even harder when asked, "Is there carpeting inside?"

"I don't know!" We were both laughing by then.

"Maybe you can show her all those pictures you took," I teased Mary because we hadn't taken any.

We love our new home and have never felt so peaceful and happy anywhere as we do here, in a Christian community surrounded by God's creation in the many trees, animals, and birds. It was so much easier to run the writer's conference while living right here on the grounds. We also enjoyed attending our first-ever Bible conference, which has been held here annually for over one hundred years.

Shortly before we moved, Mary had expressed a desire to open our home to practice hospitality, but I didn't really encourage it. Our previous home didn't feel as homey and welcoming. It's been an unexpected pleasure to entertain a dozen couples and families since moving here, along with having many deep conversations about faith. I can't wait to see what else God has planned for us here.

And yes, I do daily rounds on the golf cart we purchased when we moved here. It was only recently we discovered that the man who'd designed and helped build this cabin used to do the same thing!

DISCUSSION

But the fruit of the Spirit is love, joy, peace, forbearance, kindness, goodness, faithfulness, gentleness and self-control. Against such things there is no law. Those who belong to Christ Jesus have crucified the flesh with its passions and desires. Since we live by the Spirit, let us keep in step with the Spirit.

GALATIANS 5:22–25

1. Do you know someone you would describe as Spirit-filled? What about them displays these characteristics?

2. Which of these qualities of the Spirit do you feel are your strengths? Which qualities could use improvement?

3. Mary and Nick talk about a process of becoming more and more like Jesus in their spiritual growth and maturity, feeling the Spirit guide them. Have you felt this kind of guidance from the Holy Spirit? Give an example.

4. Does the idea of becoming holier intimidate you or excite you? Does it help to know that you don't have to "work hard" to become holier, that once you accept Jesus Christ, the Holy Spirit empowers you to follow and obey Him?

Pray together as a couple:

Lord, God, we know that by inviting You into our marriage relationship, we are also seeking a relationship with Your Son, Jesus. You have promised us the gift of the Holy Spirit. Please help our actions and words reflect this as we journey this life together in Your purpose.

Chapter 11

Commissioned

And pray in the Spirit on all occasions with all kinds of prayers and requests. With this in mind, be alert and always keep on praying for all the Lord's people. Pray also for me, that whenever I speak, words may be given me so that I will fearlessly make known the mystery of the gospel, for which I am an ambassador in chains. Pray that I may declare it fearlessly, as I should.

EPHESIANS 6:18–20

Mary:

"Maybe I'm not a Christian. I just don't get it. I don't understand what you get out of prayer or reading the Bible."

I was jolted by the words. This was a person I cared about. I wanted to see her in heaven.

I was still new in my own journey of faith, a year out from David's death, but I'd read enough of the Bible to know the way to heaven was through Jesus Christ. How could I even begin to explain what God had done in my life, how he'd changed me and was continuing to refine me through His Word and the people He'd brought into my life? Or how my prayer life had become more important than I could ever have imagined? If she didn't understand the importance of prayer or a reason to get to know God through His Word, what could I possibly say that would convey my new, personal relationship with Him?

I remember the moment but not my response. We were alone in the car for maybe half an hour. Had I defended my faith and explained my reason for hope in a way that would plant a seed that might grow someday? I hope so, but I suspect not, because I still have difficulty doing so some eleven years later.

Why? Fear. Fear of offending someone, fear of being called judgmental, fear of "that look" coming across the face of someone whose opinion I cared about. I've seen it too many times. When I began following God, I was so excited about my discovery that I gushed with my newfound knowledge. *A God who could speak to me? Guide me? Protect my heart?* I was all in. I still am. In fact, it's difficult for me to make small talk with people who don't have faith because, inevitably, I say something that gets "that look." You know the one. The shuttered eyes that no longer meet mine, or the sideways glance to someone else that means I'll be the butt of their ridicule later, or sometimes, the eye roll that clearly states, "Here she goes again."

"What helped you when your spouse died?" a newly widowed man once asked me.

"Prayer helped," I began, but he vehemently shook his head.

"The Bible," I tried again. "I found solace in reading God's Word and knowing He had plans for me."

"No. I don't want that," his tone was flat.

"I have some books by people who have been down this road and daily devotionals that only require a short read each day."

I'm a certified grief counselor, but my main go-to tool for the griever remains God, the Great Healer. I'm convinced we cannot find healing outside of Him.

"I don't want any of that."

"How about journaling?" I was desperate to help my friend in some way. "I found healing in writing about it. I have an extra journal if you want to try it?"

Again, the shake of the head. In the end, the only thing I could offer him was a listening ear. The hardest person for me to talk to is the one who openly rejects faith.

So, I hesitate. I stumble on my words, avoiding Christianese terms like "new in Christ" or "born again"—being so careful with my words to not offend when everything in me wants to shout the Word from the rooftop.

Sometimes, I think about the girl I used to be in high school, so certain of what I held to be truth. Whatever side I was on in debates was the winning one because I was so self-assured in my beliefs. In college, I wrote term papers that netted "A" grades—even when they differed from the professor's biased view—because I was that good at sharing my convictions and knew how to research to support them. Because their views *were* biased, on the liberal side, mine always conservative.

The further I continued my education, the more this proved true. In one of my master's level Family Services courses, a group was brought in to teach students how to refute the Bible-toting parents who would inevitably question some of the programs planned for schools! Another professor went through the class roster, student by student, asking how many sexual partners each one had, tallying them on the chalkboard to prove a point. What was the point? I have no idea. I was too shocked to ask. There I was, a married mother of three, the single dissenting voice in most of the classrooms. Still, I dissented. I raised my hand, questioned the professors, refused to watch a documentary that included two senior citizens having sex, even when I was threatened with failing the class if I did not look.

"Why? Are you disgusted by the idea of seniors having sex?" the professor goaded me. "Because if you don't watch, you'll receive a failing grade."

"No, it's because sex between any couple is private. It has nothing to do with their age. I wouldn't watch anyone have sex," was my reply. She couldn't force me to watch. I closed my eyes for the remainder of the film.

What happened to that young woman who boldly declared truth? I tell my husband these stories, and he calls me a "rebel," but I don't feel like one now. Yes, my whole adult life, I'd rebelled against the status quo. I had eight children, practiced a family-bed, attachment-style parenting, carried babies on my back, and nursed them until they self-weaned. I homeschooled. I wrote copious amounts of letters to the editor, decrying abortion, government intrusion into parental rights, and half a dozen other topics I felt strongly about.

Yet nothing is of more importance than our soul. Nothing has set such a fire in me as the love of God and the personal relationship that got me through the death of a spouse, the death of a grandchild, the dark nights of loneliness, the worries about raising three girls as a single mom. Nothing means more in my life than the realization that the way to heaven is through following Jesus Christ.

Jesus commanded His followers, "Therefore go and make disciples of all nations, baptizing them in the name of the Father and of the Son and of the Holy Spirit, and teaching them to obey everything I have commanded you. And surely I am with you always, to the very end of the age" (Matthew 28:19–20).

So why am I quiet? Where is that rebel for Jesus? I'm told at our annual writer's conference and in other Christian circles that I am bold in my faith. I appreciate that, but it's easy to proclaim faith among those already faith-filled. It's harder with those who don't know the gospel. Yet these are the ones we are to share the good news with.

An avowed atheist, Penn Jillette, of the magician duo Penn and Teller, posted a YouTube video in 2009 exhorting Christians to share their faith. Yes, this was from an atheist. In the video, he explained that after one of his shows, a man in a suit walked over to him, complimented the show, and, looking him directly in the eye, politely handed the magician a Gideons New Testament.

> "It was really wonderful. I believe he knew that I was an atheist. But he was not defensive, and he looked me right in the eyes," Jillette said. "And he was truly complimentary. It didn't seem like empty flattery. He was really kind and nice and sane and looked me in the eyes and talked to me and then gave me this Bible."
>
> Jillette then stated he doesn't respect people who don't proselytize.
>
> "I don't respect that at all. If you believe that there's a heaven and hell and people could be going to hell or not getting eternal life or whatever, and you think that it's not really worth telling them this because it would make it socially awkward . . . How much do you have to hate somebody to not proselytize?" Jillette asked. "How much do you have to hate somebody to believe that everlasting life is possible and not tell them that? If I believed beyond a shadow of a doubt that a truck was coming at you and you didn't believe it, and that truck was bearing down

> on you, there's a certain point where I tackle you. And this is more important than that."[6]

Powerful words from a man who doesn't even believe in God.

Nick tells me I sometimes use biblical language when I talk out loud in my sleep. I know I've said some powerful statements in my dreams. I've even baptized a couple of people! I want to be that fierce in my faith while I'm awake. Some say we bring people to Jesus by our actions, not our words, the idea being that others will see Jesus in us and want whatever it is we have.

That sounds good, but is it enough? What if they never ask what it is we have that makes us look different from the world? How will they know? I struggle with this concept, particularly when it comes to people I love. If I believe, truly believe, that Jesus is the one true way to heaven (and I do), why am I not wrestling unbelievers to the ground and forcing them to listen?

I guess it's because we can't force God on anyone. Just like Nick and I can't force couples to pray together. Our hope is that our amazing relationship is a testimony, our love story demonstrating the power of God and prayer in a marriage.

That's part of the answer; giving God glory by sharing my journey of faith and our love story. I never hesitate to share how God brought us together. Nor do I hesitate to share my individual faith story, how close God was to me in those years of grieving and single motherhood, how the Holy Spirit has guided me in the last twelve years and continues to guide me. I pray about everything, seeking God's guidance in every decision, big and small, including what words to use before I put pen to paper.

I remind myself of these words from the Bible:

> "I am sending you out like sheep among wolves. Therefore be as shrewd as snakes and as innocent as doves. Be on your guard; you will be handed over to the local councils and be flogged in the synagogues. On my account you will be brought before governors and kings as witnesses to them and to the Gentiles. But when they arrest you, do not worry about what to say or how to say it. At that time you will be given what to say, for it will not be you speaking, but the Spirit of your Father speaking through you." (Matthew 10:16–20)

Maybe that's the rest of the answer. I need to trust God to guide me as His disciple, allowing Him to use me to spread His message, knowing He will give me the words when I need them.

Nick:

My brother informed me that once I accepted Jesus Christ as my Savior, I was commissioned to share my faith. While I appreciate that, I don't always know how to do it. Mary and I moved to a Christian community in April 2024. This place hosts a Bible conference every summer. Not only did I offer my services as a courtesy golf cart driver during the conference, but Mary and I attended most of the presentations. I was impressed by a couple of speakers, a Navy SEAL and a former baseball player who knew their Bible and could recite verses from memory.

"I wish I knew the Bible as well as they do," I lamented one morning. Mary reminded me of how many country songs I know by heart and my ability to quote a line from a movie I've watched repeatedly, like "You'll have a more harmonious outcome," from one of my favorite westerns. So, I guess there is hope for me if I can recall random things like that.

I've saved a lot of souls in my dreams. In one, I stood high atop a cliff, throwing rocks with Bible verses on them. In other dreams, I've fought in an army for faith or walked with apostles. I only wish I were as strong for my faith awake as I am asleep.

It's easy to share my faith with people in our community or those who didn't know me before. What's harder is to go back to the town where I was someone else for thirty-five years and let them see my newfound faith. I'm not sure people who knew me before would believe this is the new me or even understand what that means.

An old friend of mine noticed something different about me and asked what was going on. I knew his mother, who had recently passed away, had been extremely faith-filled, so I thought he might understand my answer.

"I decided I wanted to be more like your mother was in her faith," I told him, but I'm not sure he understood, and he didn't ask questions. I hope he does someday.

"You can't change. You're a narcissist. Narcissists don't change," another person said when I told her I was a different man since accepting Jesus as my Savior. That hurt for two reasons. One, because I know the change is real. And two, I didn't think I *was* a narcissist.

I had to look up what that term meant, so I turned to "Mr. Google." According to an article on WebMD, a person might use the term narcissist to describe someone they think is self-absorbed. Well, I've already admitted I used to be self-centered, so maybe the description did fit the old me a little. However, narcissistic personality disorder (NPD) goes way beyond mere self-absorption. It's a diagnosable mental health condition, a mental illness characterized by a struggle to keep relationships, an overblown sense of worth, taking advantage of others, wide and fast mood swings, and a need for constant admiration, among other things.[7] I'm pretty sure my wife of three years would notice if I were like that, and she assures me I am not.

My previous self would have been defensive and argued my case. The new me, wrongly accused of being a narcissist, said nothing. I realized I must accept that I have no control over others' perception of me and my conversion, nor can I let their response affect my relationship with God. I had to let go of a lot of that old ego and pride to become more like Jesus. God has changed my heart. I know it, my wife knows, and God knows it, and that's all that matters.

DISCUSSION

But in your hearts revere Christ as Lord. Always be prepared to give an answer to everyone who asks you to give the reason for the hope that you have. But do this with gentleness and respect, keeping a clear conscience, so that those who speak maliciously against your good behavior in Christ may be ashamed of their slander.

1 Peter 3:15–16

1. What do you think it means to be commissioned to share your faith? Do you do that? If so, how?

2. Mary and Nick mention the discomfort they have experienced in sharing their faith stories and inviting others to follow Jesus. Do you find it difficult to share what Jesus has done in your life? Are you willing to talk about your faith even if it means getting "that look?"

3. Who comes to mind today who needs to hear the Good News? How can you reach out to them?

4. Have you memorized any Bible verses? If so, which one(s)? If not, commit to memorizing a verse from this book that resonated with you this week. Write out some of your favorite Bible verses on the blank pages that follow this chapter. Did you know you can ask the Holy Spirit to lead you to verses and help you retain them?

Pray together:

Lord God, use us to share You with others. Please give us the courage and the opportunities to share our faith, even if it scares us sometimes. Thank you for the gift of each other to walk this path of faith together. Let us be each other's encourager.

Chapter 12

Amen

Rejoice always, pray continually, give thanks in all circumstances; for this is God's will for you in Christ Jesus.

1 THESSALONIANS 5:16–18

Mary:

"I forgot to say Amen again," I lamented during our writer's conference after once again failing to end my opening prayer with the concluding word that signifies affirmation of truth.

"Maybe it's because you never stop praying," a particularly intuitive attendee commented, and I realized she was correct. My Christian faith has become so integral to my life, it's as if every breath I take is a prayer.

"Thank you for another day," is my first thought when I open my eyes in the morning. "Thank you for this man," I'll add when I glance over at Nick's head on the pillow next to mine. "Guide us in this day," I silently utter before my feet hit the floor. My journal entries inevitably include prayer. I'm not sure I ever stop praying. Not just in the big things but even in the smallest, which explains my penchant for praying before I head into a thrift store. I believe a God who cares about sparrows might delight me with the perfect discovery there: a box of stationery, a book I've hesitated to pay full price for, or the coat or pair of slacks I'd been looking for.

Most importantly for our marriage, Nick and I share prayers in the morning, in the evening, and often in between, in the car before a trip, before we make any big decision, or before an event or meeting. We've even asked God to guide our direction a couple of times during our travels and been privy to some of the most beautiful scenery as a reward for our detour. We might forget to pray before dinner, but we never forget how important it is to bathe our marriage in prayer.

We've been beginning our days with shared prayer since our second date, but it wasn't until I was diagnosed with cancer that I added praying *for* my husband, which should have been a no-brainer, considering the Holy Spirit's prompting to pray *for* him even before I met him. In the forty days between cancer diagnosis and surgery, it was Nick I worried about. He'd lost one spouse to cancer. I couldn't bear the thought of him having to face that again. I bought a book of prayers for a husband with space on the pages to write my own prayers. Nick took the book that included my handwritten prayers with him and read part of it in the waiting room.

Those intercessory prayers for Nick and our marriage helped me when I wrote them and calmed him while he read them. I've filled several other books with prayers written specifically for him since then. When I find myself worrying about his health with a declining kidney function, I turn to the power of prayer to quell the anxiety. I have no doubt God has a plan for Nick and will make sure he remains healthy enough to fulfill that plan.

There are many people on our intercessory prayer list: children, grandchildren, and friends. We have a prayer box where we add small slips of paper with prayer requests. Our morning prayers cover all the requests in the box. Occasionally, we'll go through the pieces of paper and remove those that have already been answered. Prayer boxes or bowls are our go-to gifts for any newlywed couple, along with an explanation of what prayer has done for our marriage.

I often remind Nick these last fifteen years of our lives are the most important ones because we are following Jesus and walking the path to heaven together. I'd like to think we'll have more than fifteen years together, but Nick is in his early seventies, and I just qualified for Medicare. We can't count on it. What we do count on is God will give us enough time to fulfill His purpose for our lives.

Nick and I don't know why God allowed us to have what we consider a second chance at doing marriage His way, unless it was to share our experience with others. We hope something in this book has convinced you to give prayer a chance to do incredible things for your marriage, whether you've been married fifty years or five months.

Wives, ideally your husband takes the lead in praying with and for you. That said, I've been praying this way for ten more years than Nick has, so right now, it's usually me initiating prayer during the day, but Nick is more often the one who begins praying as I slip into bed next to him. One of you is going to be more comfortable than the other leading prayer. Don't let it become an issue between you. The important thing is to do it.

Nick says:

I recently found myself agreeing with someone when they commented, "It sucks getting old," as we discussed our aches and pains and frequent doctor visits.

"It beats the alternative," Mary reminded me later. I don't have to look any further than my mother, who died at forty-seven, and Mary's grandson, who died when he was eight years old, to realize she is right.

Sometimes I forget how remarkable it was that God asked Mary to pray for me even before she knew me and before I knew Him. It was the summer after Mindy died, so I was already searching for something I didn't have in my life, but I hadn't yet changed the way I was living. To think that God cared about me even then—before I'd changed! Something amazing happened in my life when I finally figured out what was missing: that personal relationship with God. You'd think giving up an old way of living life for yourself would be a hardship, but the rewards are tenfold.

If people think being a Christian and following Jesus means the fun ends, they're wrong. I'm having the time of my life. I've never laughed so much, appreciated such simple things, or felt so much gratitude. I have a sense of peace I've never experienced before, not just because I've retired but because of that personal relationship with God.

Men, want to see a change in your marriage? Discover what a marriage centered on God can be. Praying together is part of that. I promise you; the benefits outweigh the risk of feeling awkward or stupid doing something you aren't used to.

I'm getting more and more comfortable praying. If it were a contest as to who takes the lead in our prayer life, Mary would probably take first place. But it's not a competition. Because if it was? Well, I'm pretty competitive.

I'd win.

DISCUSSION

"Again, truly I tell you that if two of you on earth agree about anything they ask for, it will be done for them by my Father in heaven. For where two or three gather in my name, there am I with them."

MATTHEW 18:19–20

1. In this chapter, Nick and Mary discuss intercessory prayer, saying prayers for each other, friends, and family. They've each written a prayer for the readers of this book. Read their prayers that follow. With their examples, keeping in mind there is no right or wrong way to practice conversational prayer, either say a heartfelt prayer out loud or use the blank pages to write down your prayer and read it out loud. Remember, the more you do this, the more comfortable you will become in praying together.

Mary's prayer:

Lord, thank you for the gift of Nick. Thank you for an opportunity to experience a marriage relationship centered on You. I am grateful that Nick has been so open to working on this book with me and open to the Holy Spirit. I pray this book touches the hearts of the readers and that our words and experiences help their marriages. Amen.

Nick's prayer:

Lord, thank you for the opportunity to work on this book with Mary, something I never imagined being able to do. I pray that our book helps couples experience what we have. I pray that my perspective as a male in a satisfying relationship helps other men in their marriages. Amen.

His

Hers

Notes

1. Don Piper and Cecil Murphey, *Getting to Heaven: Departing Instructions for Your Life Now* (New York: Berkley Books, 2011).

2. Kenneth C. Haugk, *Journeying Through Grief* (4-Book Set) (Stephen Ministries, 2004).

3. Mary Potter Kenyon, *Refined by Fire: A Journey of Grief and Grace* (Sanger, CA: Familius, 2014).

4. Gary Chapman, *The 5 Love Languages: The Secret to Love that Lasts* (Chicago: Northfield Publishing, 2015).

5. https://5lovelanguages.com

6. Erin Roach, "Atheism: Penn Jillette urges evangelism," Baptist Press (website). February 12, 2009, accessed December 4, 2024, https://www.baptistpress.com/resource-library/news/atheism-penn-jillette-urges-evangelism/.

7. Julie Marks, "Narcissistic Personality Disorder: Signs, Traits, and Tests," WebMD, February 13, 2024, https://www.webmd.com/mental-health/narcissistic-personality-disorder.

About the Authors

Nick and Mary Portzen are co-coordinators of the annual Cedar Falls Christian Writers Conference in Cedar Falls, Iowa, where they live. Nick is a former business owner. Mary is a certified grief counselor and workshop presenter. She is the author of seven books under the name Mary Potter Kenyon, including the award-winning *Refined by Fire: A Journey of Grief and Grace* and *Called to Be Creative: A Guide to Reigniting Your Creativity.* Nick and Mary speak on the topic of couples praying together. They can be reached at nickandmaryportzen@gmail.com

www.ingramcontent.com/pod-product-compliance
Lightning Source LLC
LaVergne TN
LVHW041254080426
835510LV00009B/727